CREDIBILITY MARKETING

BUILD YOUR BUSINESS BY BECOMING A RECOGNIZED EXPERT

(Without Investing a Lot of Time or Money)

LARRY CHAMBERS

Dearborn™
Trade Publishing
A **Kaplan Professional** Company

Acquisitions Editor: Mary B. Good
Senior Managing Editor: Jack Kiburz
Interior Design: Lucy Jenkins
Cover Design: Design Solutions
Typesetting: the dotted i

Published by Dearborn Trade Publishing, a Kaplan Professional Company

Printed in the United States of America

02 03 04   10 9 8 7 6 5 4 3 2 1

Library of Congress Cataloging-in-Publication Data
Chambers, Larry.
    Credibility marketing : build your business by becoming a recognized expert (without investing a lot of time or money / Larry Chambers.
      p.   cm.
    "A Kaplan Professional Company."
    Includes bibliographical references and index.
    ISBN 0-7931-4886-3 (paperback)
    1. Marketing. I. Title.
  HF5415 .C48243 2001
  658.8—dc21   2001005094

Dearborn Trade books are available at special quantity discounts to use for sales promotions, employee premiums, or educational purposes. Please call our Special Sales Department to order or for more information, at 800-621-9621, ext. 4307, or write to Dearborn Trade Publishing, 155 N. Wacker Drive, Chicago, IL 60606-1719.

■ ■ ■ ■

Contents

STAGE ONE: FORMULATION

STAGE TWO: CONCENTRATION

STAGE THREE: MOMENTUM

STAGE FOUR: EXPANSION

STAGE FIVE: STABILITY

Foreword

For most of my career, I've been focused on building a successful business. I understood the benefits of public relations and publicity—getting my name mentioned in one of the business magazines or trade publications or, better yet, having my name appear on the front page of the *Wall Street Journal*. At least I thought I understood the benefits.

It wasn't until I met Larry Chambers, who introduced me to the concept of *credibility marketing*, that I understood the power of the printed word.

Let me explain: I've spoken with many public relations firms that promised me they would generate millions of impressions by having me quoted in one of the major newspapers, magazines, or even on a national television or radio show. In the early days of my career, I hired one of the top traditional public relations firms, which was great for my ego and for my mother. But other than that, the benefits were very minor relative not only to the cost but also the time and energy commitment.

In 1992, we invited Larry to interview with our firm along with several traditional public relations firms. We were expecting to award the contract to one of the major firms, which would guarantee us exposure on TV and radio, and in major magazines. Instead, we unanimously awarded our business to Larry, who told us he wouldn't deliver any of those guarantees.

What he did differently was lay out numerous magazines and books that he had written or helped write in a process he calls *coach writing* for top financial advisors, guaranteeing that the advisors would have all the credibility they desired in their target market. He showed us that by identifying and contacting the editors of the magazines our target market would read, we would help them fill the need of publishing information from a top expert and, at the same time, position us as an expert to the readers. Credibility marketing became the major theme of our marketing plan, which has included the completion of hundreds of magazine and professional journal articles as well as three books, all significant sellers with major national publishers.

A couple of years ago, we sold our firm. We estimate that our credibility-marketing program added $15 million to the value of our firm. In fact, the company that bought us had found us by reading one of our articles.

The idea behind our credibility-marketing program was to position our firm as a provider of knowledge to our clients. Using credibility marketing can effectively position you ahead of the rest of the competition.

Larry Chambers will walk you through the steps necessary to position yourself as an expert in your target market. You need to pay attention. These ideas work if you implement them properly and can mean millions of dollars to you. Your future clients are counting on you.

John J. Bowen, Jr., CEG Worldwide founder and president

Acknowledgments

I spent most of my adult life creating one scheme after another trying to be the star; all I ever got was stress. Then one day I woke up and realized, Hey, we are all stars in our own lives. I live with a beautiful woman who loves me. I have two great kids. I live in paradise and pretty much do what I want, when I want. I'm involved in creative processes that make me happy, and my books and everything else are just the residue, the "fine ash of a really nice fire."

I want to thank Karen Johnson, a great editor and a woman of uncommon beauty; John Fox, who taught me to stop trying to control things I can't control; Mayo Morley, who will transcribe all night to make my deadlines; Rick Goeden, whose technique swimming class is the one place I can be in the moment and not have to think; the girls at Stacy's Ojai Coffee Roasting Company, who always remember my coffee order. And, to a terrific literary agent, Sam Fleshman, and Mary Good, my editor at Dearborn Trade. Thanks also for the help of William Bongiorno at Mount & Nadler.

Preface

Most people mistakenly believe that Thanksgiving has been an American holiday since the Pilgrims and Indians first broke bread together in 1621. In fact, it wasn't until more than 200 years later that one woman's campaign of words made Thanksgiving an American tradition. That woman was Sarah Josepha Hale; you know her best as the author of the nursery rhyme "Mary Had a Little Lamb."

Sarah Hale's goal was to create a permanent, national Thanksgiving Day. She used a form of credibility marketing as her strategy: she continually wrote articles, menus, and poetry that focused on her Thanksgiving themes. Then she sent reprints along with personal notes to anyone who she felt could influence her cause.

Finally, the Civil War provided an opportune time to capture national attention. In October 1863, Hale sent a letter with copies of her articles to Secretary of State William Seward, suggesting it would be "of great advantage socially, nationally, and religiously" to dedicate a day for the nation to observe Thanksgiving. Seward presented the concept to President Abraham Lincoln as a way to create national unity. President Lincoln liked the idea; four days later, he issued a proclamation forever reserving the last Thursday in November as a national Thanksgiving Day.

The basic ingredients of Sarah Hale's success parallel those that enable many professionals to penetrate some of the most difficult markets and turn business tides in their favor. This year, as you are about to carve your holiday turkey, remember how a simple writing campaign influenced a nation.

Sarah's process may sound deceptively simple; of course, it was not. I'm sure she worked hard, and it took her years to make it happen. In today's media-driven marketplace, a carefully crafted message can achieve high visibility and position its author as a credible resource overnight. My desire with this book is to impart these modern-day methods that will help you communicate your position as an expert and get your target audience to seek you out.

Whether you are a business owner, a real estate developer, an accountant, a corporate executive, a consultant, or a sales professional; whether you are financially well off or just starting out; whether your budget is the "hip-pocket national bank" or you're in command of a million-dollar ad budget—credibility marketing will work for you. Used as a primary marketing campaign or as a supplement to advertising and public relations efforts, the very process of credibility marketing will adjust your business psychology and how you see yourself in your own industry.

About the Author

Larry Chambers is a columnist and writing coach as well as the author and coauthor of more than 700 magazine articles and 34 professional business books, including 5 books from major publishing houses in 2000 alone. Two of his books remain specialty best-sellers and 3 have found their way into book-of-the-month clubs. One of his books was named one of the top 5 books for "investing on a shoestring" by Chuck Myers (Knight Ridder, Washington Bureau), and another became the basis of a History Channel special.

Chambers's firm has built a reputation in the financial securities industry for helping those who are already successful move up to the next level through writing and being published. His clients have reported growth of millions of dollars by using the same processes contained in this book.

In addition to his successful career as a writer, Chambers's background includes nine years with a major Wall Street firm, EF Hutton & Co., where he achieved an outstanding track record, including being named one of the top 20 brokers from among more than 5,000. Before joining Hutton, Chambers spent two tours as an Army Ranger sergeant with the 101st Airborne Division on a six-man Ranger/LRRP team that operated in the jungles of Vietnam.

Following his tour of duty, he attended the University of Utah, where he received both a bachelor's degree and a master of science degree and was elected to the Phi Kappa Phi honor society.

Oh my gosh, was that boring! I mean it's true; but let me tell you the real reason why I'm qualified to write a book like this. The real reason is I'm doing exactly what I'm telling you to do and it's working.

I wasn't an English major, nor did I attend journalism or marketing classes. I'm an ordinary guy who has had to overcome dyslexia. I got my training on the front lines of one of the greatest commission-based selling machines in business history—EF Hutton & Co. There I learned how to handle rejection and disappointment, and a million other items, and still come back for more. By age 30, I was living on adrenaline, coffee, and dreams that it might get easier. It never did. I had no stop switch—only forward, fast-forward, and full-speed

Inter-Office Memorandum

TO   All Account Executives
FROM   Dale E. Frey
SUBJECT   TOP FIVE PRODUCERS—MOUNTAIN REGION
DATE   November 7, 1977

The top five retail Account Executives in the Mountain Region excluding Officers, Municipal Bond Salesmen, Institutional Salesmen, and Managers are as follows:

1. Larry Chambers   Salt Lake City ✓
2. Zene Gurley   Colorado Springs
3. Yates Williams   Colorado Springs
4. Jim Parden   Denver
5. Bob Speer   Colorado Springs

Although business was slow the Mountain Region was up to the challenge as the top fifteen (15) producers averaged $17,700.00 in gross commissions. Our ability to retail Hutton's vast arsenal of products paid off in October.

Congratulations,

Dale E. Frey

ahead. What I learned back then was: If I stopped for even a moment, so did my business. So I never stopped.

Our sales office was like a demilitarized zone. Our desks formed a perimeter, and at the center of this arrangement sat the bull pit where new brokers spent hours making hundreds of cold calls until they burned out or moved up. Rows of empty desks were a constant reminder of the turnover.

About this time (1974), our nation was coming out of a terrible economic recession, and no one was motivated to buy anything, especially stocks. The only way to acquire new customers was to find new marketing tactics and strategies to get their attention. I tried direct mail and advertising, joined country clubs, learned to play golf, and attended Rotary club meetings until I realized everyone else attended for the same reason. Some of the marketing tactics worked; most wasted my time, but it was never enough. Then I was selected by my firm to attend a marketing seminar in New York with a group of blue chip producers.

One superstar had made more than $10 million in commissions that year. I followed him around all evening trying to figure out his secret strategy. As hard as I was working and utilizing every traditional marketing method to pursue prospects, I didn't see any way it was possible to make that kind of money. What was he doing different? The answer: *Everything!*

Where my approach was scattershot, his was focused. Where I needed scripts to know what to say to my next cold call, his message was relaxed and confident. While I tried desperately to convince a prospect to buy something the prospect probably didn't need, the superstar provided solutions to their problems. He had become an expert on public offerings. Companies came looking for him to take them public, and clients sought him out for his knowledge of the marketplace. He was featured on magazine covers, often quoted and interviewed, and had his own business hour on a Houston television station. He had *credibility!*

■ ■ ■ ■

Introduction: Your Gift

The premise of this book is that you have a valuable gift to offer your customers and clients: your *credibility*.

We have become a nation of do-it-yourselfers. Everyone wants to be able to do everything faster and better than anyone else. But nobody feels secure about making decisions without advice from an expert. According to today's standards, an expert is anyone whose advice appears in print, is seen on television, or is heard on the radio.

If that's not the way you are making your expertise available, then you are withholding your most valuable resource—the one product that is yours and yours alone. It's what sets you apart, defines who you are, and raises you above the competition.

You are about to discover how to present your unique perspective in a way that will change the way you market and sell forever!

INTRODUCING CREDIBILITY MARKETING

Credibility marketing is a process of positioning yourself as a recognized expert. Credibility marketing is taking what you know and getting it published in articles and magazines so (1) it's not self-serving and (2) it actually solves problems for your customers and clients. If you do that in an ongoing, committed fashion, your message will attract and keep the attention of your market.

Imagine how successful your marketing campaign would be if you could speak directly to your prospects' hearts. When a message is valued or is information that can solve a problem, people start looking forward to hearing from you. Then marketing shifts from trying to "interrupt" (i.e., intrude on) individuals to delivering something that prospects are interested in or even request, giving you a substantial competitive advantage. Although the competition continues to intrude on strangers with poor results, credibility marketers turn strangers into friends and friends into customers.

WHAT WILL THIS BOOK ACCOMPLISH FOR YOU?

If you follow the strategies laid out in this book, the marketing portion of your business will be well orchestrated, coordinated, and planned so you can move to your own unique next level. Achieving your next level could require any of the following:

- Becoming recognized as an expert
- Reinforcing relationships with existing customers and clients
- Building a self-perpetuating media publicity program
- Controlling your own publicity

HOW SHOULD YOU USE THIS BOOK?

This book provides a logical, proven, and systematic marketing process that you can either implement on your own or with help. We are going to introduce a *structure* that will address all of your marketing challenges. It's called *credibility operating stages*. These stages communicate the action items required at each step of the way, from the formulation of your new marketing process to its stability.

Because of its linear format, the book becomes a handy reference guide that allows you to easily access pertinent information, no matter where you are in your marketing process.

This chart outlines the underlying structure that will institutionalize your company's marketing and sales processes. The structure tells you where you are and what needs to happen next. It defines and determines the strategy that will best meet your marketing objectives. Specific techniques are designed with one goal in mind: to make you stand out above the crowd of competitors by strategic use of print media.

But how can you make a good impression in print media if you aren't confident about writing and know nothing about getting published? Any honest writer will tell you that the competition for getting published in today's market is overwhelming. Of course, there *is* a way.

This book will show you how to get your ideas and your name in print—and in the right place and at the right time for delivering the most effective message. I can't guarantee you will become famous, but I can tell you how to

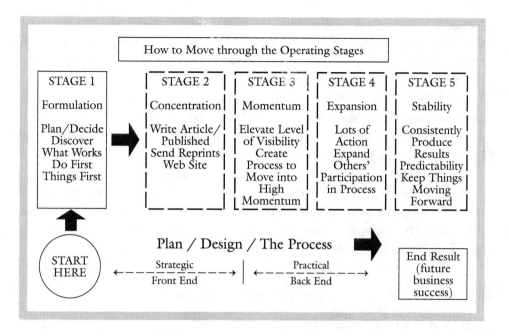

receive more visibility and enhance your significance and image as an expert in your field. And you don't have to hire a public relations firm or run an expensive advertising campaign to do it!

Stage One: Formulation

Here you learn the meaning of credibility marketing and gather knowledge of how it can be used with other forms of marketing; how most of today's news is manufactured and who the real experts are; how to develop a unique message; how to become visible locally or nationally by aligning with the media; and how to discover what every customer/client really wants.

Stage Two: Concentration

In this stage, you begin to put your plan into action. You learn how to design your message and create articles, columns, quotations, books, Internet messages, newsletters, ads, and so on. In this operating stage, you focus your attention; gather more information; correctly position yourself; tighten discipline; take small steps and complete them; and produce results. You receive a short course in why and how you should write and where you should get published. You'll discover how to write readable articles about some of the most vinegar-coated realities of business. We'll show you the steps even if you "can't write," which publications your target markets actually read, and effective ways to get an editor's attention.

You'll learn how to write the same article for multiple markets; how to prepare a professional manuscript; how to write a stay-behind piece; and what to say in a query letter to get results. You'll learn how to get published in local business newspapers and trade magazines. The book also provides examples of articles and template letters that you can personalize.

Further, you'll learn what makes a successful Web site and how to write a monthly magazine column that can be used for both print and electronic media. You'll learn how simple industry magazine reprints can become *calling cards of credibility*—and how to use these calling cards to beat out the competition.

Stage Three: Momentum

This is the stage when other people start talking about you. You become the recognized expert by integrating your program into a variety of media sources, including radio and TV. You keep doing what is working; elevate the level of communications; develop selling and marketing strategies; conduct intentional campaigns to promote your business and create demand; create a process for moving on to the next stage; and put in what's missing and, just as important, don't fix what is working.

Stage Four: Expansion

In this stage, you learn how to write a book and get it published. This operating stage expands the participation of others in your business. The efforts of this stage create a sharp rise in results.

The goal of this stage is to leverage everything you have learned and turn those magazine articles you have been writing into a full-length book that showcases your expertise. I'll reveal some important do's and don'ts, and point out relevant questions to ask so time isn't wasted writing the wrong type of book. It's possible to write a book in a short period of time by following a master plot. You will learn how to write query letters that get a response, how to write a book proposal, and how to promote your published book. You'll also be shown how to find publishers who may even pay for your marketing programs! At the completion of this level, you will understand the behind-the-scenes work of getting a book published.

Stage Five: Stability

This fifth stage is when you are doing everything you need to be doing and your credibility-marketing plan becomes predictable and produces consistent results.

For this stage, the book offers suggestions and examples of how to create and prepare for unforeseen opportunities. You learn how to make winning presentations and get the most from trade conferences. You'll learn how to convert text from your book to use in the classroom and in seminars. Best of all, by now you have begun building your reputation as an expert, so collecting names and addresses of magazines, newspapers, trade journals, book reviewers, and editors who will gladly accept your articles becomes important and will keep you well positioned in front of the public.

FORMULATION

1

The Five
Marketing Challenges

Following are the five marketing challenges you must overcome to be successful!

Challenge one: We live in a world of look-alike competitors. Because of the substantially similar choices available, it has become even more difficult to objectively select one product or service over another. The public can't tell who is competent and who isn't. And because the alternatives appear to be basically alike to the average consumer, there are no obviously wrong choices—only unfamiliar ones.

Challenge two: We are buried in clutter. Old marketing strategies don't have the effect they once did. Advertising budgets and marketing campaigns don't net the returns that make them worth the effort. Web advertising wasn't the panacea it was promised to be. Prospects, inundated by noise, tune it all out.

Challenge three: Today's consumers want to initiate contact on their own terms. If you contact them, you're thought of as a salesperson; if you do nothing, you could go out of business waiting for customers to find you.

Challenge four: Today's consumers make important decisions by seeking the advice of an expert. Even huge advertising budgets and sizzling Web sites, unaffordable to most, don't ensure you'll be noticed or believed.

Challenge five: Customers gravitate to "quicker, better, and cheaper." And unless your value is obviously apparent, prospects will quickly pass you by.

How can you even begin to step up to these marketing challenges and afford the resources necessary to compete?

Common Marketing Methods Used

The most common current, *sophisticated* marketing methods (shown in Figure 1.1) are:

FIGURE 1.1   Marketing Methods Used by Independent Financial Advisors

Marketing Method	Percentage
Passive Referrals from Existing Clients	87%
CPA & Attorney Referrals	66%
Proactively Seeking Referrals from Existing Clients	57%
Participation in Community Business	23%
Seminars	22%
Advertisements	18%
Participation in Charitable Affairs	17%
Vendor Referrals	13%
Financial Advisor and Broker Referrals	12%
Professional Trade Group Referrals	11%
Media Coverage	11%
Web Site	10%
Direct Mail	10%
Cold Calls	9%

- *Relationship marketing,* which is based on building one-on-one relationships. First, establishing trust; then, reinforcing that initial goodwill with more trust-building events. Although effective in the long run, the issue of initiating contact remains, which brings us back to the old methods of attracting attention.
- *Referrals marketing,* which is not a proactive effort but rather is making the most of what comes your way as a result of satisfied clients or customers. Referrals work great during good times, but when times turn, clients close accounts, move on, and stop sending referrals.
- *Public relations marketing,* which focuses on *media impressions*—how many times PR professionals can get your name in the press. This buck-shot approach can be expensive with any results difficult to monitor; in addition, it may not find your target market. Most public relations firms take all comers and don't specialize in one particular industry.
- *Advertising,* which is an attempt to make the unfamiliar familiar through repetition, duration, and frequency, but the costs are high and

the effectiveness low. If you asked 1,000 prospects to describe the differences between one product or service and another, the probability of anyone suggesting even one notable difference is just about zero.

To the public, advertising claims are largely unbelievable. Added to this skepticism is the fact that traditional advertising manipulated consumers by using shame to influence and persuade a buying decision. Little wonder that consumers maintain a defensive posture.

- *Direct (database) marketing.* Direct marketing is just not effective for reaching today's smarter market. A 2 percent response (in any industry) is considered good, but that means you were rejected by 98 percent of your target audience. No one likes being on somebody's target-market list. Today's consumers want to initiate contact on their own terms, when they need or desire your service or product.

Traditional Interruptive Marketing

I recently overheard one of the top executives at a major investment firm telling an associate how he built his business. "It's simple," he said. "You get on the phone and call, call, call. I wouldn't hire anybody who won't make cold calls." Why is he still doing what worked 20 years ago? Because he doesn't know anything else. Traditional marketing tactics taught service professionals how to pursue prospects mostly through *interruptive contact,* either directly or indirectly.

Marketing used to be simple. There were three television networks and the local radio station, a few well-known magazines, the Sunday *New York Times,* and the U.S. Postal Service. Consumers were frequently interrupted at home and at work by telephone solicitors. Today, consumers simply say to unwanted callers, "Take me off your list." And if they call back, they could be fined. Now, cold calling, direct mail, and media advertising have all become aggravating, shame-based, look-alike background noise.

And how have most marketers responded to this new era of marketing? They just keep raising the volume, creating more noise and clutter. They're aware of the barrage of ad clutter; but, by golly, they're going to be at the top of the heap! Even if it doesn't make them any more appealing than the rest of the heap.

Have you noticed that car sales ad announcers on the radio are always shouting and talking faster than speeding bullets? They believe if they can get their message out loud and fast, they can make us listen. I don't know about you, but I just click these commercials off.

And it's not just radio advertising. The same holds true for television, direct mail, print, and online advertising. Products and messages get lost behind publicity stunts, shock tactics, and sex and/or romance. These tactics don't produce the results they did even a year ago; yet the increase in the number of advertising dollars is staggering (see Figure 1.2).

Online advertising has grown from next to nothing in 1996 to $8.2 billion in 2000. Cable TV had revenues of $14 billion in 2000 and the mighty magazine advertising business's total revenues were $17.7 billion in 2000—another record year. Of course, we understand why: Although no one knows exactly what marketing effort will work, everyone believes increasing the size—whether of volume, frequency, or cost—will make the difference. It's easy to understand why those who can afford to do so have insulated themselves so they can't be easily reached.

There's an endless and expanding universe of new products, urgent solicitations, money-back guarantees, discount prices, and faster services. Audi-

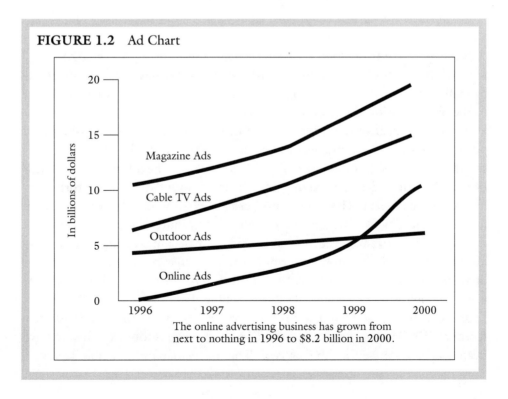

FIGURE 1.2 Ad Chart

The online advertising business has grown from next to nothing in 1996 to $8.2 billion in 2000.

ences have become fragmented and divided; the media are in just as much trouble as the advertisers. Cable TV ratings are eroding the networks' ratings. At the same time, TV commercial interruptions are at an all-time high—16 minutes for every prime-time hour.

Consumers react defensively to being inundated. We narrow our focus. We mute commercials, screen phone calls that we don't want to receive, and delete e-mail unopened. Print ads seldom get read either.

The average reader spends 25 minutes looking at a consumer magazine. Three of the top national magazines, *Forbes, Fortune,* and *Worth,* carry an average of 90 ads per issue. Let's say you don't read any of the articles, just the ads—that's less than 27 seconds per ad. Hardly enough time to justify an average cost for a full page at $100,000!

To survive the onslaught of marketing noise, our psychological defenses take over. Have you noticed that you're not aware of the sensations of your clothing against your skin or the pressure of your legs against the chair? Your brain has learned that these signals are unimportant and don't require attention during your current activity.

How does your brain know when something is important?

Selective listening. We take in information selectively. We listen more intently to information that supports what we already believe than we do to information that refutes what we believe. Our minds also have a reactive pattern to the way some information is delivered.

A study of reactive behavior was conducted on turkeys using a simulated polecat, the turkey's natural enemy. When approached by the simulated polecat, the turkeys went into a rage. The researcher tried the approach again, this time with a tape recorder making the cheeping sounds of a baby turkey attached to the polecat. This time a mother turkey gathered the cat, along with her cheeping chicks, underneath herself. The minute the tape ended, the turkey viciously attacked the polecat she had just been nurturing. This behavior, in psychological jargon, is termed a *fixed action pattern reaction* and is demonstrated most automatically around issues of survival. And the behavior is just as common in humans! "Gobble, gobble."

Humans have many fixed action pattern reactions; one of them is *selective listening.* I'll bet you have accused your children or spouse of this or have been accused yourself a time or two. This particular human trait seems to have been specially programmed to meet the challenges of today's information overload.

Indeed, automatic behavior is more prevalent today than at any other time in our history because it is the most efficient form of behavior. We live in the most extraordinarily complex environment than any that has ever before existed on this planet. So what do we do when technology moves so fast that our nervous systems can't process all the stimuli? We find shortcuts; we revert to automatic defensive reactions; we shut down or withdraw.

We can't possibly recognize or analyze all aspects of life we encounter daily. We don't have the time, capacity, or knowledge, so we often default and use rules of thumb or stereotypes to classify things according to a few features and then respond mindlessly when one or another of these triggers is present.

Some nights after a long day in the writing studio, I'll spend half an hour in front of the television just channel surfing. Even if I have my eyes closed, the minute I hear John Wayne's voice, I feel safer. John Wayne is not going to let the plane crash or the Indians get past him. Two voices in the world do that for me: John Wayne and Vince Scully, the sports announcer. I associate the tones of their voices with these assuring words, "You can relax 'cause I'm in charge and everything's under control."

It's human nature to want to believe that someone is driving the bus. Someone is in charge and everything is going to be all right. This is why we react the way we do to an authority figure or an expert. They gobble, gobble, and we don't have to think; we react automatically. Authority figures and experts have a high place on the social ladder in our culture because their position gives the impression that they have superior access to information and power.

One of the best examples is the way we perceive physicians. Because our health is so important to us and a physician has such a large amount of special knowledge and experience, physicians are among the most highly respected authorities in our culture. In the past, no one overruled the doctor's judgment—except perhaps another doctor of higher rank. For years, a long-established tradition of automatic obedience to doctors' orders has held sway.

We use information we get from an authority or expert as a shortcut for deciding how we're going to act in a situation and what we might purchase (*Influence: The Psychology of Persuasion,* by Robert B. Cialdini).

Some time ago, the late actor Robert Young counseled people about the dangers of caffeine for a commercial recommending caffeine-free Sanka brand coffee. The commercial was highly successful and sold so much Sanka that it ran for years. Why would anyone be so influenced and take an actor's word for the health consequences of decaffeinated coffee? The advertising agency had hired Robert Young because they knew that in the minds of the American public, he was Marcus Welby, M.D., a role Young had played in the popular, long-running television series of the same name. Gobble, gobble, react!

We now live in a world where most information is less than 15 years old; scientific knowledge is said to double every 8 years, and because 90 percent of all scientists who ever lived are working today, the doubling is likely to continue. We travel more and faster, change employment more often, relocate more frequently to new residences and new locales, come in contact with more people of different cultures, and have shorter relationships. We face an array of choices among products unheard of in previous years and that may be obsolete or forgotten by the next few years.

The array of product choices explains how we've developed our ability to collect and store and retrieve information. The ordinary person now holds staggering amounts of information, more than Einstein would ever have dreamed of. But more and more frequently, we find ourselves in the position of having to narrow our attention and shorten our responses to particular pieces of information, which can lead us to erroneous actions or the fixed action patterns of animal behavior discussed earlier.

At a financial seminar, I asked the group I was addressing if they knew how to find a financial advisor. One woman responded, "Oh, yeah, just look in the back parking lot for the most expensive car. Then go inside and find out who owns it. That's the advisor you want." In reality, you might be better off with the one who hasn't yet reached that level of success or doesn't exhibit her success in the type of vehicle she drives. In any case, the type of car she drives would hardly be a qualifier for a good financial advisor, but isn't such stereotypical thinking the most efficient shortcut to a decision?

Such shortcutting is also part of the mechanism the brain uses to tune out repetitive stimuli or signals that have no immediate value. For example, people living near railroad tracks or airports learn to ignore the sounds of trains and planes. Likewise with advertising messages, there is little or no discernible difference to the public. The quality of products and services has improved so much and commodities are so interchangeable in the minds of consumers that it doesn't really matter which product or whose service or business they use. We tune out intrusive and irrelevant messages . . . until our need becomes immediate. Then we choose what's handy. It's just human nature.

GOBBLE, GOBBLE, REACT!

Take an objective look at your marketing brochure, Web site, business card, or oral pitch to prospective customers. I'll bet your marketing tools look or sound just like—or are similar to—your competitors'. The point is that you are filtered out before you have the chance of being seen, heard, or read. The prospects you do win are mostly a matter of the odds.

The underlying problem is that *you can't persuade prospects or earn customers' loyalty until you first have their attention*. And we can no longer assume that we are getting customers' attention just because we inundate them. Consumers are tired of having the one commodity that they should be able to control—their time—continuously interrupted.

Permission Marketing

Permission marketing shuns interruptive messages in favor of first obtaining prospects' permission to contact them. When prospects give permission, they are willing volunteers who want to learn more about how to participate in your product, class, seminar, or service.

The way to gain prospects' permission is by trading something of value— information, solutions, service, or some form of entertainment. When you deliver a message that resonates with, and is of value to, prospects, they, in turn, look forward to the communication, and control over whether to contact you is placed in their hands on their time schedule.

The secret to a successful marketing program is aligning your approach with the way prospects want to be sold. Unless you've built a permission marketing program that motivates prospects to look for you, you can only expect to get the same paltry percentage of responses to your efforts that all your look-alike competitors are getting. It's time to change direction!

■ ■ ■ ■

2

Credibility Marketing

Credibility marketing is a powerful methodology that shifts the effort from persuasion and customer acquisition to loyalty and customer retention. Used correctly, it attracts the right kind of customer by delivering a message that informs and provides solutions calmly, without shouting or appearing as just another one of the competitors.

WHY USE CREDIBILITY MARKETING?

The heart of credibility marketing is to establish your message as an expert opinion and give prospects a reason to pay attention. It is based on communicating a viable solution to a need or problem, thereby creating recognition among qualified prospects. Deliver enough informative messages and you heighten your prospects' level of interest, while your competition continues their interruption campaigns with poor results.

Credibility marketing turns prospects into willing volunteers seeking what you have to offer. Rather than a one-way monologue, credibility marketing becomes a two-way dialogue with self-selected, preendorsed, and prequalified prospects.

Imagine how successful your marketing campaign would be if you had something original to say or your message was read by 95 percent of your target prospects—not the 2 percent who respond from direct mail or the 5 percent who read consumer magazines. If your message conveys valuable information that can solve a problem, people start looking forward to hearing from you. Compare your own emotions when receiving a welcomed and anticipated personal phone call versus your feelings when receiving a cold call during dinnertime. Instead of annoying interruptions of our privacy and time, credibility marketers trade something of value for the consumer's attention: a service, some form of new data, or instructive information.

What Not to Do

Marketers go in the wrong direction when they try to impress prospects with how much they know and by using industry jargon. But jargon doesn't communicate very well. The analogy would be a number of American Ph.D. physicists listening to a Japanese physicist talk about physics in Japanese. The Americans wouldn't understand a word, but if the Japanese physicist spoke English, they'd all get it. That's true in your world also. If you use the jargon of your trade when you write and speak, your listeners won't understand what you are talking about. So write and speak in a way people can understand without talking down to them; the result is they feel good about themselves because they're understanding a subject they thought was very complicated. Then they feel good toward you subliminally because you're the one who's making them feel good.

THE PROCESS OF CREDIBILITY MARKETING

Figure 2.1 shows what credibility marketing looks like as a process. You begin the credibility-marketing process by gathering extensive knowledge about your own profession or industry, by evaluating the unique needs and challenges that affect your customers, and by packaging your services and products to show how you can address your customers' concerns. Along the way, you develop media contacts and third-party endorsements from the press, and publicize magazine articles or books you've written.

Credibility marketing does take skill, patience, and effort to develop. You can't go from anonymity to a trusted leader overnight; it's a process that grows exponentially over time. But the rewards of shifting the focus from persuasion to invitation, from mistrust to trust, and from unfamiliarity to loyalty are well worth it!

FIGURE 2.1   The Credibility-Marketing Process

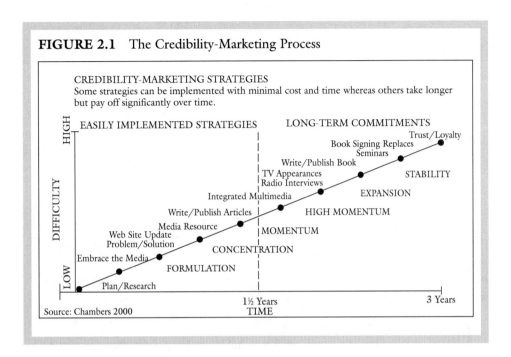

CREDIBILITY-MARKETING STRATEGIES
Some strategies can be implemented with minimal cost and time whereas others take longer
but pay off significantly over time.

Source: Chambers 2000

3

Embrace the Media

Have you noticed that writers, journalists, and reporters have become experts by default? No one questions their, or their editors', qualifications or possible biases. No one stops to consider that most of these people have little or no knowledge and/or experience in the areas they write or report about. They've usually spent years learning the fine art of journalism. So why do readers believe their information, trust their opinions, and follow their advice? Because it's there in black and white! And the popular assumption today is that anyone whose advice, opinion, or information appears in print is an expert.

What the media present has been filtered through the slant of the reporter's or writer's or editor's unique perceptions of what he's seen or what he's been told or what sells.

HOW FAR CAN YOU TRUST THE MEDIA?

The news is only the lens that frames the image of the object, not the object itself. Added to this is the fact that the majority of "news" is manufactured (see Figure 3.1), and most stories are sensationalized to keep your attention so that sponsors and advertisers can sell you their products. They can also get things wrong!

FIGURE 3.1   How the News Is Generated

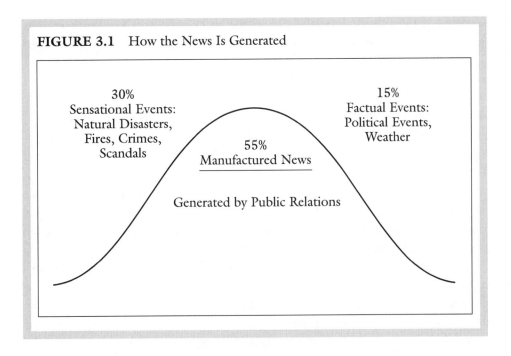

The media provide unqualified recommendations and endorsements—any corrections and retractions go unnoticed. Advertisements can be easily recognized and dismissed, but a headline, a quote, or simple commentary can influence readers' disposition and emotions and stimulate action even if it's wrong or unproven.

Millions read or listen to every word from media "experts" and make decisions—from what movie to watch, how to dress for the weather, or what route to drive to where to eat. People rely on the media as their key source of information about drug risks and benefits, although a new study published in the *New England Journal of Medicine* (2000) warns that media coverage of new medications often overstates the benefits or overdramatizes the risks. And seldom are any financial ties disclosed between the media's sources of information and the new medications.

Another example of media misinformation from Wall Street is the media's dramatization of the 436-point stock market drop on March 13, 2001: "Historic Dive on Wall Street" covered the entire front page of *USA Today*. Verbs like *crashed, sank,* and *plummeted* were used instead of *dropped* or *declined*. It's never "stock prices moved lower"—no, they "*fell* into bear market territory."

Someone arbitrarily decided that when the stock market fell below a certain number, it meant we were in a bear market. But less than a month later (April 6, 2001), when the Dow Jones Industrial Average rose 402.63 points, what were the headlines? "Tiger Woods Chases Pack!"

The golf headline is an obvious example of how writers and journalists receive a following not commensurate with their level of expertise on the topic of investing. I'm sure you can recite inaccurate or unproven headlines involving your own industry that influenced consumers' opinions and/or decisions. This is not to imply that journalists and reporters are irresponsible. In fact, reporters' reputations depend on the quality of their stories. Most media have fact checkers; but they would also readily admit the pressure to fill their pages and maintain and improve their standings. They thus spend most of their resources creating appealing content.

In contrast, you study the needs and problems of your market, you understand the trends in your industry, and you model your advice, service, or product to best serve your clients or customers. The media will never, in a lifetime of reporting on your industry or profession, be able to match the level of knowledge you acquire by running your business day-to-day.

HOW TO BEST USE THE MEDIA

The various media need interesting articles, timely news stories, a fresh angle, and credible people to interview. They want your knowledge of industry innovations and trends. Why not become their resource? By providing data and research, you give reporters the valuable gifts of credibility and accuracy. Keep in mind that it's a two-way street: the publication of your ideas, opinions, and activities acts as a powerful third-party endorsement to your benefit!

Because credibility marketing occurs primarily through print, it's time you learn how to communicate with the people who are going to facilitate your status as an expert. Lets look at this from a writer's perspective. The media are dependent on advertising to pay for production and distribution. Advertisers place ads only in respected media within their selected markets. What makes a certain form of media respected is the quality of its stories. Quality stories depend on quality sources. The media need experts to provide insight, knowledge, and accuracy. Experts arouse the interest of the audience, which draws in advertisers. You, as the expert, are fundamental to media economics.

Writers and reporters are always in a hurry, always up against a deadline, and always looking for a lead story. Their stories determine their reputation and space allocation, so they need someone like you to fill in and explain details, provide a fresh angle, add dimension, and corroborate their findings. If you relieve their pressures and provide consistent, reliable information, you will become the trusted expert they call first.

The Local Approach

A frequent question I hear from new clients is, "Can you get me published in one of the national consumer magazines?" I have to explain that it's more advantageous to get into a trade magazine like *Ocular Surgery News* or a client's local business review. National consumer magazines are almost all staff written, whereas most trade publications have only a small, or no, writing staff. In addition to being initially more receptive to your submission, you'll probably receive more qualified consumer response for your effort.

Although *Ocular Surgery News* has a circulation of only 60,000, the readership consists mainly of ocular surgeons, whose average net worth is more than $2 million and average annual income $500,000. This means that virtually every subscriber is a prequalified wealthy prospect. Submissions that address the particular concerns of that readership will be well received, and authors will be positioned well in their target market.

In addition, an article or speech directed to your local business community that provides new information and/or solutions will generate inquiries from other media. The national media often find stories by combing through the regional media, and the broadcast medium finds stories by combing through print.

So before you pitch a story to the *New York Times,* make a name for yourself in the minor leagues. Pitch your alumni magazine, trade journals, local business papers, and Web sites, all of which are anxious for content. Rather than targeting a national publication, start by approaching local business journals, the business section of the local newspaper, and your town's chamber of commerce and Rotary club newsletter publishers. Clients' frequently asked questions and concerns create patterns that can be turned into dynamic story ideas for a variety of media.

Assemble evidence of your reputation as a reliable resource. In public relations parlance, build a "media kit"—*not* a press release! Rather than an advertisement about yourself, your product, or your service, create a publicity portfolio that includes articles written by or about you or your quotes from interviews. Then use your media kit to create enduring visibility!

Align with the Media

- **Building relationships with the media.** It's important to learn how to communicate with the people behind media technology. Understand their difficulties, pressures, and needs, and you will be the trusted expert they call first.
- **The media need you.** You can be the media's expert source. The various media need your knowledge of industry trends. You follow and understand trends in order to serve your clients or customers. The media will never, in a lifetime of reporting on your industry or profession, be able to match the level of knowledge you acquire by running your business day-to-day.
- **Client questions and concerns.** Clients' frequently asked questions create patterns that can be turned into dynamic story ideas for print and electronic media.
- **Analysis and research.** By providing data or research, you offer TV and newspaper reporters credibility and accuracy.
- **Industry contacts.** Be the "source of sources." Get to know other experts and introduce them to the media.

■ ■ ■ ■

4

Are You *In*visible?

Let's suppose you made the local news with the announcement of someone's promotion to vice president or the opening of a new office, but because the response to the news had no effect on business growth, your visibility quickly faded. Perhaps you are interviewed and your opinion is quoted; you could circulate copies as long as the topic remained pertinent. Likewise, for a while you would make a mark with a single article written by you or about you, your service, product, or process. You might even get the article reprinted by another publication and so extend its life. You see . . . the goal is to showcase your expertise in a way that builds lasting visibility.

LEVELS OF VISIBILITY

The broad base of the visibility reach pyramid in Figure 4.1 consists of the invisibles. When you land here, no one knows who you are no matter how much expertise or experience you have. It's only when you move off the bottom rung that we begin to notice your talents and start to think of you as an expert. On the next level, you may never need to go beyond your own geographic area. Then there are the experts who have talk shows on local channels or write regular monthly newspaper columns. They are followed by regional celebrities whose names reach beyond their immediate area. The

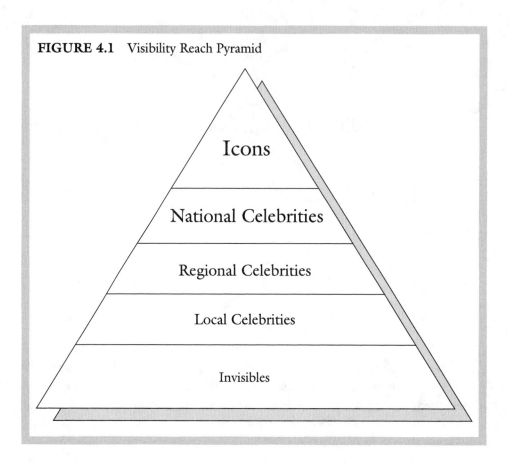

FIGURE 4.1   Visibility Reach Pyramid

Icons

National Celebrities

Regional Celebrities

Local Celebrities

Invisibles

higher levels thin out rapidly, until only a few people are left commanding the highest visibility. They are also the most highly compensated.

Some people in your local community are more visible than others, including leaders of the community's major institutions: the leading banker, business owner, investment advisor, lawyer, physician, football coach, and politician. The local celebrity process is fueled by the local media's constant search for stories to tell.

In the past, most local celebrities didn't seek visibility; they acquired it as a by-product of their occupation and lifestyle. Now, local celebrities are increasingly turning to professional image consultants and marketing professionals to help improve their visibility. They're aiming for higher levels of visibility, and many end up leaving their community to seek a wider audience. You need to assess whether you are content to be a regional celebrity or aspire to having business from all over the nation. Both can be rewarding.

Every major city contains well-known people who fan out beyond its borders. Regional celebrities are drawn from the ranks of business leaders, fashion trendsetters, and small-college athletes. Regional celebrities who aspire to higher visibility can use their regional visibility as a stepping-stone to national, even international, visibility. Some people make the jump from regional to national celebrity, not by climbing the ladder within their sector, but rather by crossing over to a more popular, active sector.

One of my clients, Michael Lane, began operating on a regional level but was elevated to national visibility by writing trade magazine articles and books to help the public understand his product. He used his enhanced visibility to establish himself in the national press. One of the major companies in his industry became aware of his expertise, followed his success in the press, and made him an offer he couldn't refuse when the timing was right. His reward: he now is director of advisory services at TIAA-CREF, a multi-billion-dollar financial services company.

The highly visible in most sectors are frequently well known only to members of those market sectors. The industry icon who makes an emotional connection develops a reach that spreads like wildfire across diverse market sectors. Superwoman of the icon empire is Martha Stewart—she didn't invent good taste but she stands for it. She is the classic celebrity speaking to the psychological needs of the mass media with the merchandising skills of Michael Eisner. What Martha Stewart sells is a guarantee—the simple concept at the base of her success. She's built an empire from her home catering business to books, magazines, syndicated newspaper columns and television programs, and merchandising—all the way to Kmart.

Another household name is Richard Simmons, who became an expert by building a fitness and weight loss empire. His advice wasn't that novel or necessarily better than anyone else's, but he's sold millions of dollars worth of books, videos, tapes, and diet products. He did it through constant exposure over a broad media base. For a while, it was nearly impossible not to see him on talk shows, sitcoms, infomercials, or at one of his over 200 annual personal appearances. He started with nothing more than an investment of time and energy.

There are one-day, one-week, and one-year celebrities as well as permanent legends. Reporters create one-day celebrities daily, but most are submerged into invisibility again shortly after. A well-prepared one-day celebrity can turn this limited coverage into unlimited mileage through reprints strategically positioned in a marketing program. Greater reach and longer duration translate into greater fame and reward.

The point: Most professionals outside the realm of sports remain invisible because they're not aware of their fate. The last thing on their minds is promoting themselves. Most simply have a reactive sales strategy that only sells referrals once they've walked in the door. If you are planning to last in your profession or business, you're going to have to change such an approach entirely. You are going to have to at least give some thought to your own visibility or lack of it. Think visibility in everything you do, from the moment you plan your credibility campaign to how you make initial contact with a prospect. Everything should be coordinated and directed to increase your visibility.

LOOK FOR OPPORTUNITIES TO MOVE UP THE VISIBILITY LADDER

Sometimes things drop in your lap. The Mir spacecraft was scheduled to crash down on March 23, 2001. A week earlier, Taco Bell hired a boat, went to the South Pacific, and relatively inexpensively placed in the ocean a large floating sheet—a target—with the Taco Bell logo on it. It advertised a challenge that it would give everybody in the United States a taco if any part of the errant space station hit the Taco Bell target and even took out an insurance policy in case it happened. Taco Bell was the talk of every newscast and late night comedy show for days.

You don't have to go to such an extreme as Taco Bell did to climb to higher visibility. Here are a few easy suggestions for gaining visibility:

- Think how what you provide could be expanded to solve other needs or prevent future concerns of your existing customers.
- To become visible, you must let people know you're in business. Send notices to trade associations in which you might want to become involved. Such associations usually publish specialized trade magazines and newsletters, which are an effective way to keep track of news, people, trends, and up-and-coming events.
- If you join an association, don't fade into the woodwork; become an active member. Attend conventions, trade shows, seminars, and other networking meetings. When you are perceived as "one of them," your audience is especially receptive to your message.

- Develop your Web site into a resource that your prospects want to "bookmark" for regular reference.
- If you are an active participant in an association or industry, sponsor awards, contests, or scholarships that give others recognition and help them grow in their professions. Send press releases to local broadcast and print media promoting awards you or your company has sponsored. Emphasize an activity other than yourself or business so you're not perceived as "just in it for ego."
- Enter competitions. Send a notice of your winning results to your local media.

Such activities might not immediately show on your balance sheet, but they will help you gain recognition as a leader in the community—an image you definitely want to project. If you are modest or think becoming visible is a bit over the top, then change the way you think about promoting yourself. Don't just jump on the latest bandwagon. Find something you can get behind—a charity or award or social problem—and represent it. Simply deliver much-needed information to an audience starved for solutions.

SIX SIMPLE STEPS TO HIGHER VISIBILITY

Early on in my business life, I came across a visibility mentor. This guy was systemically closing multi-million-dollar deals while the rest of us were having trouble paying the mortgage. At the time, what he was achieving was virtually unheard of. His initial strategy was to collect any current articles about his prospects' business issues and send out copies along with a personal cover note. He also wrote how-to articles and got them placed in the local papers and his clients' business magazines. He then sent reprints of these articles to selected prospects so that he was not perceived as a salesman (as I was) when he called on them. His attention was not on himself but on the current problems his target market was facing. He possessed knowledge important enough to be published, and he was careful to leave a trail so he could be found.

I have paraphrased his six simple steps in the way I have used them:

1. Decide you are going to become an expert in your industry and then research everything about it. Build a library of facts, not just sales literature.

2. Determine just who your market is. Write out a profile of your ideal customers or clients.
3. Next, research the common problems being faced by customers and clients in your industry.
4. Find solutions to these problems. This may take research and time, but the rewards are extraordinary. Interview outside your field, if necessary, for answers.
5. Become a source for your local media. Position yourself as the messenger of solutions to the problems you found in your industry.
6. Build a system (e-mail or slow mail) to continually send out relevant information/articles each month with a personal note.

All of these steps involve learning how to articulate what you have to offer in terms so simple that a prospect can easily understand and remember. And the way to do that is to make what you have to offer applicable to prospects' issues. Make it about them—not about you. You don't even have to own the solution—just be the messenger!

Keep in mind that you're focused on standing out from your competitors (gaining visibility) and being perceived as an expert (having business come looking for you). Just because you know your business, do a good job, and consider yourself successful by your own terms doesn't ensure your future success and a growing market share in your industry. That can occur only if you remain visible as a *messenger of solutions*. This doesn't have to become a new vocation but should be a natural outgrowth of your interest in meeting your market's needs and solving its problems.

■ ■ ■ ■

5

Position Yourself as a Messenger of Solutions

Positioning is generally considered a defensive strategy. When you position yourself against your competition, you invite comparison. That's probably not going to be in your best interest in all situations, but, in any case, it also makes you part of the clutter.

Most marketing consultants teach positioning as the art of controlled perceptions; but the attention is still on you. Credibility marketing calls for a new approach, a different perspective: *position yourself as a messenger of solutions to your market*. This takes the attention away from what you have to offer and puts it on what you stand for.

EXAMPLES OF SOLUTION MESSENGERS

The concept of positioning yourself as a messenger of solutions to your market became clear to me a few years ago when I was conducting a successful ten-city seminar program around the country. I began each meeting by asking a few participants to tell me what they did for a living. Without fail, the introduction was always the same; each would say his name, job title, and company name, and some just handed me their business card.

Finally, one participant had a different answer. He said, "Hi, I'm Rob Taylor; I help successful Silicon Valley executives solve complex business and personal problems as they relate to the business, so that they are able to spend more time with their families." I watched others in the audience react to what he'd just said. This man had positioned himself in the minds of everyone present. He had identified his target market, where his marketplace was, what he did for them, and what the benefit was to them!

I was once at a Rotary club meeting where new people were asked to introduce themselves and their line of work. One man volunteered, "Hi, I'm George, a hypnotherapist. My specialty is assisting dysfunctional people in the local community." I noticed that none of the group was motivated to run over to this guy after the meeting, but I don't think they forgot him very quickly—I never did.

THE IMPORTANCE OF A BENEFIT STATEMENT

A carefully thought-out *oral benefit statement* can position you in two important ways: it turns off the people you don't want to work with and turns on the ones you do! You want to attract the attention of the people who fall into your area of expertise. And you don't want to waste anyone else's time—particularly yours.

Does your oral benefit statement compel the right people to seek you out? Does it set you apart from your competition and position you as the expert? Is this a turnkey positioning statement you can use with everyone you meet?

With today's technology and media, the world is a smaller place and everyone is more sophisticated than was true just a few years ago. People want to quickly eliminate anything or anyone not applicable to their needs and desires. You seldom get a second chance to persuasively articulate your position.

WHAT *NOT* TO SAY OR DO WHEN MAKING A BENEFIT STATEMENT

When you meet someone for the first time and ask what he or she does, and that person answers, "I work for the best company . . . we have the best performance/service/product," are you skeptical, disbelieving, and dismissive? I am.

Imagine you are about to make the biggest presentation of your life and you're allotted only 20 minutes. You are competing with three of your biggest competitors. They're good, very good. The prospect wants to understand more about you, about what you do, and why it should hire you over these other professionals.

Winging It versus Preparing

You don't have time to ask the prospect a lot of questions. This tosses you a curve as your style is to wing it, and you've even taken great pride in the challenge of making a presentation off-the-cuff. But today you're facing competitors who have been polishing their presentations for months. They have all the collateral sales material: articles, booklets, and Web sites. They don't wing it.

Can you articulate your business and personal background in a way that is compelling and differentiating? The way you respond to this question offers an immediate impression to someone regarding your confidence. The way you answer sets up trust and builds rapport.

Begin by introducing yourself. Explaining for whom or for what organization you work is typically done by giving organizational history, strategic alliances, relationships, and length of time the business has existed. If appropriate, provide the name of the department in which you work and explain the role of your department or group within the larger organization. In addition, provide your professional and personal background, if appropriate (i.e., how many years you have been in the business, with whom you were formerly affiliated, any professional designations, and where you went to school).

Imagine you walk into the same room, but this time you're prepared. You've worked on your verbal positioning statement. You've done your homework. Now you look around the table, develop eye contact, and say something like this:

> Ladies and gentlemen, I want to thank you for the time that you've allotted me today. I want to respect our time limitations, so in the next 20 minutes I'm prepared to describe what I believe you want to know about me. The first issue I'll address is who we are by telling you about some of our accomplishments and areas of interest. Second, rather than just *say* what it is that we do, I'd like to hand out several articles we've authored that *show* you what we do. Each article solves particular problems inherent in your industry. I believe this will answer a number of your questions. Third, I'd like to tell you with whom we've done business and how they have benefited.

And fourth, I'll detail what you can expect in a working relationship with me and my organization.

Now I'm sitting up and taking notice! Spend some time pondering these four suggestions. They may give you a renewed sense of confidence, passion, and speed that will enable you to connect with prospects or existing clients in ways that will take your business to new heights.

FOUR KEY ELEMENTS OF AN ORAL BENEFIT STATEMENT

1. Keep it short, simple, and concise. Think of riding in an elevator or being at a cocktail party when somebody asks, "What do you do that helps your clients and/or customers?"
2. Relate to something already on the prospect's mind. What are the prospect's goals? What is of common concern?
3. How does what you offer solve a problem or need for the prospect? Write out three problems you can identify on a three-by-five-inch index card. Then write down solutions to those problems. How do you solve everyday business-related problems like those your clients have?
4. Develop a strong promise or benefit you can say when you are introduced. Mine is: "I get all my clients published."

The key is to focus on a specific niche of your market rather than trying to solve all problems for everyone. The narrower the niche, the easier to understand the unique needs of a specific market. For instance, if you sell course books to schools, you might say, "I work with school book stores, monitoring their buying habits." It can be that simple.

A Shortcut to Preparing a Statement

Another way to write a positioning, or benefit, statement is to borrow from successful ones. Go through business magazines and pull out advertisements that catch your eye. Separate the ads by service or product categories. Choose the ad copy that you feel makes the best statement for each category. Then try adapting the concept, theme, or syntax of the strongest ads to your own situation. You want your message—your positioning statement—to resonate in the market you are trying to attract. Use the following questions to help form your positioning statement:

1. Who are you?
2. What business are you in?
3. What people do you serve?
4. What are the special needs of the people you serve?
5. With whom do you compete?
6. What makes you different from your competitors?
7. What unique benefits does a client derive from your service?

After you've taken a stab at your positioning statement, ask yourself these questions: What is it that I really do? Does my message tell the world what it is that I do? Do I feel confident and passionate about it?

Make all your collateral material consistent with your positioning. The first thing most people want to do is have a glossy corporate brochure printed with everything matching, as if that's the magic silver bullet. Yet one of my clients, who has almost $2 billion under management, doesn't have a formal corporate brochure. In fact, he never mails any marketing or sales material—especially anything that's glossy and looks like mass marketing—because that's sure to turn off affluent prospects.

You can find a million different ways to present your services to an individual prospect but usually only one or two *effective* ways. Try a couple of variations and start using your benefit statement in your conversations. If you're writing newsletters, add your statement. If you are to be interviewed by your local newspaper, use the opportunity to tell readers who you are and what you do.

Make notes on how you can put this advice to work in your daily encounters. For now, set this chapter aside; you'll be coming back to use your benefit statement in later chapters.

■ ■ ■ ■

6

Does It Really Work?

MEASURING THE VALUE OF MARKETING PROGRAMS

Most public relations and marketing people measure sound bites, print impressions, and eyeball exposures. They measure actions they control, but that's a distorted view that has no way of measuring responses. It's like doing pages of homework instead of one thing that has value. If you want to find out if your marketing approach is working, ask your customers, "Does my Web site have any value to you?"

One simple way to measure TV or magazines results is to direct activity to your Web site. Ward Hanson, Stanford Business School professor and director of Stanford's Internet Marketing Project, is conceptualizing an intriguing approach to online media measure that he calls Web chains. A Web chain describes all possible sequences of events that may occur as a result of an online exposure, and Hanson has developed a metric measurement for each branch of the chain.

In magazine articles, you can use a simple thing called a "call to action," whereby you monitor the number of incoming calls generated by your invitation. An approximate return can be calculated for every ad campaign—online, TV, radio, or magazine. The entire marketing communication program then becomes a unit, not just a single, footprint of attention.

Several years ago, one of my clients, a financial industry association, aka the Institute, wanted to undertake a marketing program to increase membership.

Some of the group thought that advertising was the appropriate way to get new members; others thought offering courses was the best method; and others believed in direct mail to their target market. What I offered was my credibility-marketing program.

All of the marketing methods were sampled simultaneously in four different publications. The responses were tracked so that anytime anyone called the Institute, the respondent was asked from which publication he or she had learned about the Institute. A more detailed tracking report is shown in Figure 6.1, which provides for a variety of sources.

In the past, the organization wrote down the names of those calling and added them to their data list for notification of meetings and conferences. When a caller became a member, no one knew how the contact was generated because many marketing programs were running at the same time. After the organization started keeping records, the callers could be identified and tracked back to the magazine and even to the specific article.

The results of the study were surprising. In a ten-month period, my firm's PR article had generated 3,919 leads in four categories versus 813 inquiries for all other media programs. Overall, our finding for this form of PR outperformed all other forms of advertising in that particular period by a 5-to-1 ratio. When a strong compelling message hit home, coupled with an offer such as a free booklet explaining the subject in depth, the article outdid advertising by a 15-to-1 ratio.

My associates and I wrote an article about a particular problem and included an offer: "For more information, contact the organization for a free guide." The editor allowed us to put in the phone number and address. The phone number wasn't even a toll-free number and still in one month we had over 900 prequalified responses. During the same period, other programs were averaging 10 responses but most had none. The name and address of the callers were recorded and a mail campaign installed. Direct mail was then effective because we had a list of self-selected prospects. That year the organization's membership doubled, and it tripled over the next four years.

We also discovered something else surprising. The number of responses picked up whenever we offered free booklets: one on how to build a business, another on marketing, and the last—from which we had more than 950 responses—on how to protect your personal liability, which helped brokers in presentations to clients. The extra persuasiveness was that what each booklet offered was clearly relevant. This was an accidental finding—we had just wanted to see how many people had inquired about the Institute.

FIGURE 6.1   The Institute's Tracking Report

Month   March 1996

	Week 1	Week 2	Week 3	Week 4	Totals
Member Referrals	7	8	25	17	60
Registered Rep	153	146	102	335	736
Financial Planning	6	1	8	15	30
Associate Member	3	7	11	2	23
A Free Booklet	8	9	7	2	26
CPA Course					
Tapes					
Annual Conference	28	25	20	12	95
Special Mailers					
Other					
Total	205	206	176	383	970

The results (shown in Figure 6.2) were an overwhelming response of 3,919 inquiries from articles we'd written giving advice compared with fewer than 813 responses through traditional methods, word of mouth, referrals, direct mailings, and advertising!

You should stop and think about all of this for a bit. How does it fit your business plan? My goal was to convince you this stuff really adds value before moving on to the action steps in the next sections.

You are now going to shift gears to a new operating stage (concentration) in Section II. I hope you have already begun to put your plan into action. Next, you will learn how to find the right forum for what you have to say—articles, columns, quotations, books, Internet messages, newsletters, ads, and so on. In this operating stage, you'll focus your attention; gather more information; tighten your discipline; take small steps and complete them; and produce a result.

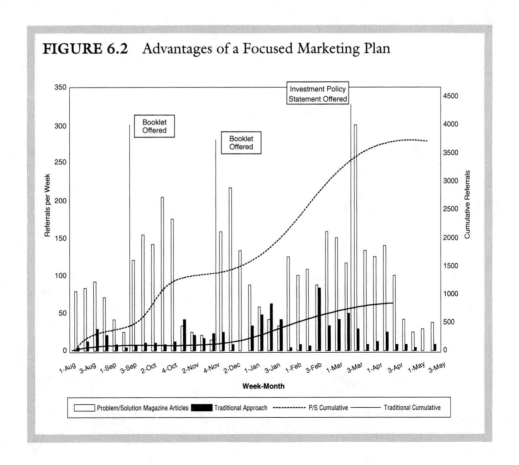

FIGURE 6.2 Advantages of a Focused Marketing Plan

STAGE TWO

■ ■ ■ ■

CONCENTRATION

■ ■ ■ ■

7

Get Started!

Great! You've decided to take credibility marketing to the next level. This chapter is a marketing plan template that can keep you on track as you implement the tools of credibility marketing.

STEP ONE: GATHER INTELLIGENCE

Becoming an expert carries with it the responsibility of being aware, informed, and accurate. You need to know everything you can learn about your area of expertise and keep that knowledge thorough and up-to-date. Hone your research skills. Get to know others involved with your markets. Discuss their concerns, needs, and desires, and let them know yours.

STEP TWO: IDENTIFY YOUR MARKET

Your ideal market is not dictated solely by what you have to offer. Think about your own preferences and with whom you enjoy working. Begin with a study of your existing customers/clients—who they are and what their commonalities are. This should help with identifying and expanding your best markets. Identify centers of influence—people in key positions within organizations you are targeting—and consider forming strategic alliances with them.

STEP THREE: FOCUS

After selecting a market, specialize. Each market has specific challenges; discover where the real opportunities are for what you offer. Select an area of concentration or a specialty. Zero in on the common concerns or problems in that area. Determine how what you offer can best be used to resolve these concerns or provide solutions to the problems.

STEP FOUR: DEFINE YOUR MESSAGE AND POSITION

Determine the most compelling benefit statement for your particular market. Your message should indicate your ability to solve problems and position you as the source. Make a habit of identifying unique problems to your target markets and of developing solutions to those problems. Look for opportunities or new areas that need to be addressed.

STEP FIVE: COMMUNICATE YOUR MESSAGE

Get the word out. You have to communicate the benefits your company is uniquely positioned to provide to the right people (see Figure 7.1) at the right time through the right channels to be effective.

Discover the most effective way(s) to communicate your message and be seen. Simply having your name or picture appear in a magazine or in your local newspaper is hardly more than an ego boost and of very little value. Your ideas need to be published and broadcast. The secret to my success has been to find trade magazines that would accept my work and publish it quickly.

Become an active member of an association, and don't fade into the woodwork. Sponsor awards, contests, or scholarships that give others recognition and help them grow in their professions. Such activities may not immediately

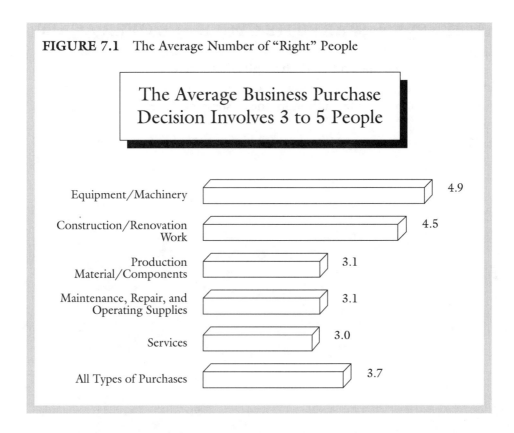

FIGURE 7.1 The Average Number of "Right" People

The Average Business Purchase Decision Involves 3 to 5 People

Equipment/Machinery	4.9
Construction/Renovation Work	4.5
Production Material/Components	3.1
Maintenance, Repair, and Operating Supplies	3.1
Services	3.0
All Types of Purchases	3.7

show on your balance sheet, but they will help you gain recognition as a leader in the industry and the community.

STEP SIX: MEASURE YOUR PROGRESS

Set up systematic reviews of your marketing efforts. Create a visual display. This will create momentum, strengthen your vision, emphasize successes and achieved goals, and help you stay on your marketing track. Ask yourself these questions:

- Where can I make my market program stronger?
- What more can I do?
- Is my approach achieving the results I want?

STEP SEVEN: START THE CYCLE ALL OVER AGAIN

Go back to step one and work through all the steps again. This is an ongoing process that leads to becoming a recognized and respected expert. Expertise is earned over time, although these steps will help you shorten the process.

What do you do now? How do you break in? Where do you go?

■　■　■　　■

8

The Reprint Tactic

Remember that you don't have to be the author of an article. You are the messenger of solutions.

SOURCES FOR GENERATING BUSINESS

As a writer who has focused on the financial services industry, I scour the industry's trade journals for trends. The biggest trend during the past 20 years has been the move from commissions to fees, which affects every aspect of the industry's world. If I didn't know that, I wouldn't have very much credibility among its ranks.

Trade Publications

I have clipped a collection of articles from trade journals over the years that I can refer to on every possible subject in the financial services industry. I spend a short time each month skimming a variety of publications. Whenever I find a pertinent article, I send it to a client with a brief note—only a sentence or two. I had a preprinted pad made up at Kinko's that reads "I thought you would find the enclosed article of interest" along with my name, address, and phone number, plus enough room to write a short note.

It takes so little time, and the expense is minimal. A published piece from a periodical that educates, informs, or solves a problem can be very effective in generating new business. The message my client receives is that I understand the problems and concerns he faces. It says you are taking the time to be on the lookout for your client's best interest, and that translates into enormous goodwill and credibility.

The Internet, News Bureaus, Trade Editors

Research the Internet and news bureaus for material, or contact editors of trade publications to tell them what you are doing and to ask for suggestions or information about what's relevant to their readers. You may establish an important strategic alliance with the editor of your local newspaper or business journal, who may ask you to write a piece or inquire if you would be amenable to an interview.

POSITIONING YOURSELF AS AN EXPERT

Sending out reprints, handing them out to customers, and leaving them with prospects is an effective way to tell clients and prospects you're not just a product pusher. That fits with the concept of positioning yourself as an expert in an industry. Because people respond favorably to an informed professional offering a solution to a real problem in contrast with a salesperson pushing a firm or product, I've listed the following ways for you to impress clients and prospects with your professionalism:

- Look for news or similar items that support your opinion and/or what you have to offer.
- Clip pertinent items, noting the article's title and publication information (publisher and publication date), and send copies with a brief note to your prospects and clients.
- Keep a copy of items you send in your reference folder for helpful information when you begin your own writing.
- Contact the publication for reprints of full articles that merit sending to a larger mailing.
- At a minimum, send out a recent magazine or newspaper article once a quarter.

Example of a Perfect Reprint

TECHNIQUE WHITEWATER
BY MARY DERIEMER *contributing editor*

Sit Up Straight

Correct posture will improve your safety, power, and balance.

It seems so basic element, yet it's one of the most important things you can do for your paddling. Upright posture allows us to access our full range of motion. This leads to greater balance, more power and safer body positions, whether upright or upside down! So let's look at what it takes to do this and some tips to help us improve.

Sit up in your boat by arching your back slightly and pushing your navel toward the front of the cockpit. Feel your pelvis roll forward, your knees and thighs press up under the deck, and your spine grow taller. Viewed from the side, your straight back has a slight forward cant. A couple of physical limitations to truly sitting up straight are flexibility and outfitting. If your hamstrings and lower back or your outfitting is tight, you won't be able to realize your full potential. Flexibility requires a stretching program, and it takes weeks before the results are felt. You can fit stretching into your day while watching a TV program. Be sure to warm up the muscles first to prevent injury and get the most from your efforts.

If your outfitting is too tight, it can inhibit your best posture. Some seat designs encourage a slouched position. You can add foam to the back third of the seat to change the incline. If the seat tilts forward, this assists with the arch in your back and helps roll your pelvis forward.

Balance and range of motion are a function of posture. Try these simple drills to experience what that means.

■ In your kayak on a flat pool of water and without your paddle, hold your arms out to your side as you sit up straight.
■ Go wild and rock your boat as much as you can from side to side using your hips. How is your balance? Your range of motion?
■ Continue to rock the boat as you lean forward. What changes do you notice in your range of motion—more, less? How about your stability?

■ Now, lean back so that your spine makes contact with the cockpit coaming as you rock your hips. What happens to your range of motion? Your balance?

Think about what you discovered; your greatest stability is found sitting upright or leaning slightly forward. Your greatest lateral range of motion is found sitting up straight. Nothing worth repeating is found while leaning back! Now, which posture do you want to use in the rapids? Sit upright, and during those moments when you think you might flip, arch forward.

The increase in range of motion that you get from sitting upright includes torso rotation. The large muscle groups of your torso are your greatest source of power, but only if you use them! The more you rotate, the more power is available to move your boat.

This torso rotation plays a big part in avoiding injury as well. Especially when you're doing strokes that start or end toward the back of the boat, rotation will allow you to keep your hands and elbows in front of your chest, thus reducing the risk of shoulder injury.

LEAN FORWARD to practice torso rotation and see how much more power and flexibility you develop.

Drill

■ Sitting in your boat with your new upright posture, rotate your torso and look at your back grab loop. How's your rotation?
■ As in the drills we did earlier, check out what happens to your rotation as you lean first forward and then back.

It is important to note that arching forward or back allows for a great deal of rotation, while permitting you to affect the pivot point of the boat on the river. Arching maintains the posture that allows you to use your full range of motion. Slouching forward or leaning back decreases your ability to rotate fully and negatively affects your stability.

Until you are naturally flexible, your body will tell you that it's fatigued from all this perfect posture. Give yourself a rest! While you're drifting downstream or resting in an eddy, relax. But as you peel out to enter that rapid, sit up!

Mary DeRiemer has been teaching and guiding since 1982. DeRiemer Adventure Kayaking offers classes and trips in the western states and Ecuador. □

Source: Canoe & Kayak, July 2001. Used with permission.

Wes Fall, a commercial property manager, followed my advice and began sending reprinted articles to qualified prospects in his area. The reprinted articles pointed out problems that occurred only in high-tech industry properties—for example, loss of electric power, bike pathways, parking—and suggested how to address these industry-specific problems. One particular property owner was so impressed with what Fall knew about the industry that the owner felt confident Fall was the perfect manager for his properties. The result: the owner transferred over a multi-million-dollar project to Fall. The property manager now sends out articles every month!

The reprint tactic keeps you in frequent touch with your key customers and contacts. Don't give them a chance to forget you! *Repetition* is the key to gaining audience recognition. And *consistency* is the key to inducing customers/clients as well as prospects to associate your name with *expert*.

The reprint practice has long-reaching benefits. It's something you can do easily and for little or no cost, no matter what other marketing efforts you are using. Best of all, it will prepare you for writing an article and even suggest where you could publish it!

9

Print Media

THE NEED FOR FREELANCE WRITERS

For as long as magazines have been published, consumer and trade editors have relied on freelance writers to supply the words. Albert Einstein, Eleanor Roosevelt, Tom Peters, Ken Blanchard, and Harry Houdini have all freelanced for magazines. The demand for freelance magazine writers has remained strong and has especially today; the reason is economic. Magazines have become more and more specialized, and as a result, smaller circulations can't afford to maintain the large editorial staffs they once had to keep their pages full. They turn to freelancers—and trade publications do so even more.

When you follow the credibility-marketing outline for writing articles and submitting them to trade, or even consumer, magazines, in effect you're borrowing from the noble tradition of the freelance writer. This tradition is also one of the reasons why the techniques you're going to read about work.

Actually, you are going to be competing with freelance writers. Professional freelance writers may have the benefit of knowing the inner workings of magazines, but they also get paid for their work. Their living depends on the words they write. You have an advantage because you're going to give away your articles. Your payment is the third-party endorsement you receive from being in a particular magazine or trade publication. Your agenda is to further your career or to attract prospects to your business. Don't lose sight of this fact. It is your strength.

My objective was to get my articles published in industry and service trade magazines. I was under no delusion that I might be the next Ernest Hemingway. In fact, if you want a prescription for failure, establish perfection as your goal. If you keep to the fore the reason you're using writing and the value of being published, you won't run into trouble.

GETTING STARTED

Where do you begin? I started by buying a book similar to this one and read it until the pages were worn. I studied articles in magazines and thought about why I enjoyed certain ones more than others.

Obviously, you want to aim at getting into publications that your prospective customers/clients read. It's not *People* magazine in the reception area. It'll probably be magazines you've never heard of, such as *Dirt and Rock, Medical Economics,* or *Cemetery Management.* For example, in the doctor's front office you'll find popular mainstream publications, but in the back office you'll find *Ocular Surgery News* and *Diversions.*

Next, if you investigate where the top 100 companies advertise, you'll learn a surprising fact. The largest business-to-business advertisers in the United States collectively spent $3.36 billion in 1997, and trade magazines are the number-one favorite medium for getting messages to potential customers. Consumer magazines rank far behind as number two. To succeed in a brand-conscious world, advertisers go where research tells them to go. Copy their tactics.

You still want to write for a mainstream magazine like *The New Yorker, Fortune,* or *Money?* Don't waste your time. These publications have writers on staff. You'd be competing against them as well as against professional freelance writers. In addition, these publications strive to appeal to broad markets, not special interest groups.

If you have a good idea, you'll find that the editors of trade publications are more accessible and sometimes even help you tease out a good story, even though they know you're not a professional writer.

FIGURE 9.1   Consumer Magazines versus Trade Magazines

National Consumer Magazines

- Reach less than 2% of target market
- Huge readership
- Entertainment
- Staff written
- Full-page ads $100,000 per one-time placement

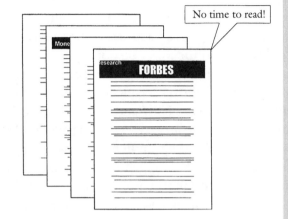

Industry Trade Magazines

- Reach 95% of target market
- Industry credibility
- Education
- Industry trade readership
- Freelance writers welcome
- Full-page ads $10,000 per one-time placement

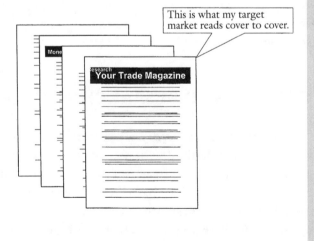

COMPARING CONSUMER MAGAZINES WITH TRADE PUBLICATIONS

Although they have a huge readership, national consumer magazines reach less than 2 percent of any niche target market. Their stories are primarily for entertainment, and because they are staff written, freelancing is discouraged. In addition, a full-page color ad costs well over $100,000 today in these magazines.

Now look in the lower box of Figure 9.1 at industry trade magazines. Because they are written for a specific industry, they reach 95 percent of that market. Although readership may be tiny in comparison, trade magazines enjoy industry credibility and, best of all, freelancers are encouraged to submit articles. Trade magazines have smaller budgets, which means they have to take talent where they can find it. Many times they either don't pay their writers at all or pay only a stipend. Trade magazines are a terrific place to gain experience and accumulate good clippings.

And if you are an advertiser, you save tens of thousands of dollars. A one-time full-page, four-part color ad in *Newsweek* averages $167,000 an issue, whereas the same-size ad in *Bloomberg Wealth Manager* costs less than $8,800 (see Figure 9.2).

Advertising also provides clues about who reads a particular magazine. Are these readers your target market? If they're 30-something singles and you're marketing to 50-year-old mid-western families with four kids, you may be wasting your time. If the magazine is pitching luxury automobiles and jet planes, your article titled "Ten Steps to Finding a Pediatrician" may be going to the wrong market.

FINDING AND RESEARCHING TRADE MAGAZINES

Look for the *Encyclopedia of Associations* at your local library. There are over 23,000 associations, with new ones starting all the time. Each college or university has an alumni magazine; so you can ask the reference librarian for the book that lists these magazines. The directory I recommend highly is *Who's Who in Association Management.*

If you don't have access to a library, you can purchase media directories from Burrelle's (800-631-1160; <www.burrelles.com>); Bacon's (201-992-6600; <www.baconsinfo.com>); or Gebbie Press (914-255-7560; <www.gebbieinc.

FIGURE 9.2 Why Trade Magazines? Cost Comparison

	Circulation	Cost for full-page, four-part color ad
Consumer Magazines/Newspapers		
Newsweek	3.1 million	$167,380
Wall Street Journal	1.8 million	154,000
USA Today	2.6 million	123,000
Money	1.0 million	115,370
Fortune	650,000	95,000
Forbes	750,000	83,210
Trade Magazines		
Registered Representative	91,500	$14,873
Financial Planning	100,000	9,575
Investment Advisor	73,000	9,295
InvestmentNews	61,000	8,835
Bloomberg Wealth Manager	45,207	8,750

com>), among others. You can reference *Gale Research,* which lists thousands of associations and their newsletters and publications (800-877-4253).

Spend an afternoon at the library flipping through the publications on your list, or send for sample copies. You should get a feel for the content, format, editorial slant, and tone of each. You'll want to write your articles to fit the style of the particular publication and medium. You may even write different versions of one article for different media.

Check out magazine covers; they tell a lot about whose attention the magazine is trying to attract and what it believes readers are interested in. Does it favor articles that relate to your product or service? Does it address men, women, or both? Old readers? Young readers?

Study the table of contents. You'll usually find a list of what's included in the first ten pages of the magazine. Notice what issues are being presented and see if there could be a slant to your product or service that might help that particular industry.

You'll also see bylines, which will tell you whether the magazine leans heavily toward well-known writers or if it is open to newcomers. A quick comparison of the bylines in the table of contents with the names of the staffers listed on the masthead can tell you whether the magazine is staff written or freelanced.

Every magazine has a masthead. It's the first page I read because it gives me the name, address, phone number (usually), and e-mail address of the editor I can query. Here are some of the job titles you'll see starting from the top:

- The *editor-in-chief* is usually the person in charge of the editorial part of the magazine. If it's a smaller trade magazine, that's the person to whom I address my queries because he or she is likely to pass it on to the appropriate editor.
- The *executive editor* may be in charge of other editors but may not work directly with writers.
- The *managing editor* is often in charge of scheduling and working with freelance writers, but in my experience managing editors mainly do all the follow-up work for the executive editor.
- For a larger magazine, the *articles editor* is the best person to query. Others, such as the *editor-at-large, associate editor,* or *assistant editor,* have varying degrees of authority; they may not work directly with freelancers and would only pass your article on.

Check if there's a regular department in the magazine that covers your particular specialty. Is there a regular column or are there a variety of writers? Are articles staff written or freelance? The *Writer's Market,* which comes out every year and is sold in local bookstores, tells you which magazines use freelance writers and the percentage of articles that are freelance written. The higher the percentage, the greater the chance you have of getting your article in that magazine.

You also want to look at the articles because they provide hints of what the editor likes and accepts; reading them gives you an idea of the magazine's format. Are the articles mostly "how-to"? Are there biographies? Is the magazine primarily a news publication?

Here are a few things you can learn by reading a few of the articles. How do they begin? Do they use anecdotes? Are they news flashes? Is there some lead that's titillating? Are any articles humorous? Do they have sidebars? Does the magazine run seasonal articles? How long are the articles in general? A quick way to estimate is to count the number of words in an average paragraph and multiply by the number of paragraphs.

Magazines change criteria and staff quickly. Experience has taught me that editors who start with small magazines move on to bigger magazines as their career progresses, and they take their best writers with them. When the old guard is gone, new editors may be open to your ideas.

There are some 900 new magazines launched each year, according to the University of Mississippi's journalism department, which compiles an annual guide to new magazines. Half fail in a year and only three out of every ten will be in business in four years. But they all need writers—lots of them. New magazines are especially receptive to new writers for a couple of reasons. One is obvious: they don't have a large network of writers yet. Usually, their budgets are still small and they'll take a chance on less experienced writers. How do you find these? Check newsstands and talk with your clients about what they're reading.

HOW DO YOU BEGIN? WHAT SHOULD YOU DO?

The same process that works for a freelance professional writer will work for you. Start by approaching an editor with a story idea in the form of a *query letter,* which is discussed in detail in Chapter 10. Sometimes this process is reversed with well-known professional writers; the editor approaches them, but in most cases, your tactic is to write your ideas in a letter. If an editor likes your query, you will be assigned the story; the notice usually arrives in a letter or e-mail confirmation. It covers such things as the length of the article, the deadline or due date, and payment (if any). Some agreements go into detail, but it's been my experience with the trades that a verbal agreement is more likely. I've had a lot of luck just by calling up editors and getting into a conversation to find out what they need and then asking if I could submit an article.

Let's say an editor has given you four weeks to complete an assignment. What happens next? While you're busy planning your article, the editor has probably given your article much thought—not so much how it will turn out but how it will fit into the production schedule and other articles being lined up. In January, for example, the editor may be reading final proofs for February, editing manuscripts and approving layouts for March, April, and May, and making assignments for June. Your article simply fits into a pipeline, so it isn't necessarily going to get a lot of attention just yet.

The next step is sending your completed manuscript to your editor, where it may sit for days or weeks while deadline matters are attended to. I found that one way to get an editor's attention is to send everything by priority mail—that moves it up a little higher on the pile.

Picture a room filled with manuscripts, magazines, and query letters in addition to stacks of still unread articles. Most editors still like to read from a hard copy, so they print out manuscripts submitted by e-mail. If your article looks fine on the first read, it is sent around to other editors or other staff for their comments. If it needs more work or if it's light in one area, the editor might suggest a rewrite. If it's beyond repair, you may just get a rejection. But I've found that most editors, no matter how bad an article is, will give me a second chance to repair it.

Maybe the editor is basically satisfied with your idea but may return it for you to strengthen some parts. Veteran freelancers expect this—new writers are shocked by it. The veteran writer feels it provides a chance to rebuild and polish the article. With the request for a rewrite usually comes a new deadline, sometimes only a few days or weeks away. Meanwhile, while you're working to rewrite or reedit your article, the editor is packaging it for publication. The editor may be talking to the art director about the layout or artwork, or photographs may be assigned. One of the first articles I wrote ended up being a cover story, and I worked with the art director on the picture that would best convey the theme of my article.

The editor will also probably retitle your article with a focus more on the publication's market. That's why I don't spend a lot of time on fancy titles; out of 700-plus articles I've written, very seldom does one of my original titles make it into print. Spend your time on the article instead.

This is also the time to put together your credibility-marketing "bio," which I mentioned earlier in the context of your verbal positioning statement. How do you want people to think about you when they read your bio? Here's where you put in your name, how to contact you, your e-mail address, any Web sites, and one or two sentences about what you do and how you solve problems for your clients. The editor will sometimes ask for a photo.

You may find out that you'll be involved in some form of the production right up to publication and possibly even afterward. Many magazines do fact checks. If you send in a chart from a source other than yourself, you may need to have a release or permission to use it. A copy editor may be assigned to your article and may resubmit it to you for final approval. A copy editor focuses on such details as spelling, punctuation, grammar, and style as well as illustrations you may want to use.

Some magazines also send a galley proof of your article. At this stage you can see what it's going to look like and fix any remaining errors. One of the big ones for me has always been misspelling someone's name. Nothing is worse than to go to all this trouble, get in print, and have a principal's name misspelled.

Possible Problems and Pleasures to Anticipate

The editor could decide your article is six lines too short, so the assistant editor calls and asks you to insert an additional 200 words. Or the article may be three lines too long, which would justify some trimming. You get the article back and find that the very meaning of the article disappeared on the editor's floor, so there may be a last minute rewrite.

Finally, everything is approved, the article has been placed in a layout, and all finishing touches have been added: the headlines, subheadlines, miscellaneous elements, any quotations or blurbs, and/or such inserts as sidebars. Along comes publication day. You may discover that you are the last one to receive a copy of the magazine. Everybody else will have seen it, read it, and called you about it before you finally receive your free copies or find it at the newsstand. A consumer magazine—a November issue, for example—may appear in the last week of October, whereas usually subscribers get their magazines beforehand.

But your job isn't over yet. Now you must call the reprint department for reprint copies of your article. The magazine owns the copyright even though you're the author. Permission to use the article normally comes from the publication, but the reprinted article just may be your new brochure or your credibility calling card. Rather than running off copies on your copy machine, you should try to get a good buy on reprints from the reprint department. In most cases the department will put your name, title, phone number, address, and e-mail address on the title page of the reprint.

The cover page of the magazine is the front page of many reprints, which adds to the credibility of your article. Four-part color, graphs, and your photo may also show up. For you to replicate this in a brochure would cost thousands of dollars, while for a dollar or two per reprint, you'll be able to use these for many years.

THE QUERY LETTER

The critical ingredient of the submission process is the query letter—literally, a letter of inquiry. Why send a letter? Why not just send a finished article? It's a debate. I've done both and I've had success with both. With a larger consumer magazine, it's almost mandatory to send a letter.

The query letter is a simple one-page document that proposes the article, states who the author is, and makes a short case for why the readership would be interested. A one-page query letter has no more than three paragraphs. What is the article about? What are your credentials? And what's the potential market? Choose your strengths and devote an entire paragraph to them. The query letter really needs to be perfect, because the well-written letter is your best shot at seeing your article published. So work on it until it looks right; this isn't the time to dash off a quick note. It's an example of what the editor's going to see in an article.

WHERE CAN YOU GET GREAT IDEAS?

Behind every article within a magazine is an idea. But where do ideas come from? Remember that as an expert in your profession, you have an advantage over most writers. You are constantly solving problems for your customers and clients. You know their concerns—and those concerns are the very reason they're reading the editor's magazine—which makes you more attractive compared with an ordinary freelance writer. Read everything you can get your hands on, keep up with the field, and see how different stories and ideas fit with your products and your services.

Books are also a great place to come up with article ideas. See what's selling at the bookstore. Fresh ideas appear first as book titles and make their way to magazines—and vice versa.

Old magazines are another source for an idea folder. You can check the library for past issues. It's a rule of thumb that articles are recirculated about every five years. You'll start to see a pattern. Don't spend a lot of time doing this, but old magazines are a great place to find initial ideas.

Newspapers in the industry are yet another place to discover local trends that can be widened into an article idea or problem to be solved. Keep the scissors handy, cut out articles, and drop them into a folder.

The Web is another time-saving as well as time-wasting place to look for article ideas. It's great if you can find a magazine site with useful articles, but you have to search out the good things on the Web, which takes time.

Conventions have focus groups or panels that discuss problems in an industry. You can jot down some of these ideas to use for your article. And tap into your own experience. Chances are you've been solving problems or working with customers and clients for a number of years. You may have done research or have personal experience that you take for granted. Jot down ideas. Keep a journal. Don't take anything for granted. Editors are looking for good ideas, but not all editors are alike and not all of them are going to think the way you do. Sometimes something you take for granted might be an incredibly valuable idea that could be turned into a story.

Maybe your competitor has already done the story you've come up with. That's why it's good to check back issues of several publications to see if the topic's been touched. The Web and your library can make this task a breeze. An editor may consider an idea "old stuff," or he may have just run a similar article in the previous issue. There are thousands of magazines—if one editor can't use it, another may.

UNDERSTANDING YOUR RIGHTS AS A WRITER

One-time rights pertain to selling your magazine piece. An editor may ask for North American sale rights. If you send your article to a trade magazine, that magazine will normally have North American serial rights even though you haven't been paid. These rights simply mean that you're giving the magazine the right to publish your article for the first time in North America. The word *serial,* incidentally, is just a fancy name for magazine.

Once the article has been published, you may be able to take it elsewhere. The next magazine contract may call for second serial or one-time rights. Again, you're simply selling or giving the rights to publish your piece once, and then you'll be able to sell it again if you wish.

Some magazines, normally consumer magazines, are not satisfied with just the right to run your article once and will require all rights. They want to be able to use it in another magazine, a book, a videotape, an audiotape, or on the Internet—any medium that they're working with. Obviously, the North American serial rights, or one-time rights, are the best arrangement for you.

Because many publishers now have electronic versions of their magazines on the Web and commercial online services, they may ask for electronic rights. If you sign an all-rights contract, the magazine can post your article online at will. Again, it's a matter of remembering what your focus is. If it's credibility marketing, you want your article posted everywhere.

If a newspaper, for example, wants to reprint a piece of your article, the magazine contract may cut the magazine in for a portion of the reprint fee. A 50-50 split between the writer and the magazine is common, but if you were to sell all the rights, then the magazine could sell it and you'd get nothing. Again, it's a matter of where your priorities are.

Your contract may include an indemnification clause, which means that you're on the hook financially for any legal action. You're wondering why, when the magazines normally are the deep pockets? Mostly, it's just to scare you into being extra careful about what you say.

Additional Resources for Getting Published

Magazines

- Camenson, Blythe. *Your Novel Proposal from Creation to Contact: The Complete Guide to Writing Query Letters, Synopses, and Proposals for Agents and Editor.* Cincinnati: Writer's Digest Books, 1999.
- Cool, Lisa Collier. *How to Write Irresistible Query Letters.* Cincinnati: Writer's Digest Books, 1990.
- Daugherty, Greg. *You Can Write for Magazines.* Cincinnati: Writer's Digest Books, 1999.
- Digregorio, Charlotte. *Beginner's Guide to Writing and Selling Quality Features.* A simple course in freelancing for newspapers and magazines. Portland, Oregon: Civetta Press (503-228-6649).
- Gage, Diane, and Marcia Coppess (Contributor). *Get Published: Top Magazine Editors Tell You How.* New York: Henry Holt, 1994.
- McKinney, Don. *Magazine Writing That Sells.* Cincinnati: Writer's Digest Books, 1994.
- Ohi, Debbie Ridpath. *Writer's Online Marketplace: How and Where to Get Published Online.* Cincinnati: Writer's Digest Books, 2001.
- Wilson, John M. *Complete Guide to Magazine Article Writing.* Cincinnati: Writer's Digest Books, 1993.
- Yudkin, Marcia. *Freelance Writing for Magazines and Newspapers: Breaking In Without Selling Out.* New York: HarperCollins, 1993.

Journals

- Shulman, Joel J. *How to Get Published in Business/Professional Journals.* Plainview, N.Y.: Jelmar Publishing Co. (516-822-6861).

10

The Successful Query Letter

Before you spend a lot of time writing an article, let's find out if there is a market for it. You do that by writing a query.

A query letter can pave the way to a receptive editor or redirect your efforts to a more appropriate department or publication. It has four main functions: (1) it must sell your idea, (2) sell you, (3) save you time, and (4) motivate you. The motivation comes once the article idea is accepted for publication. You'll find the time to write it.

Number one, and most important: get the editor's name right. I've seen great query letters addressed to "Dear Editor," which ended up in trashcans. Know to whom you are writing—have a copy of the publication by your side as you write your query letter.

Number two: neatness counts. In addition, everything in the query letter must be accurate: spelling, grammar, facts—and especially the name of the magazine. The good news is that the letter doesn't have to be very long. It should be short and direct. Introduce yourself and ask for the opportunity to present your article ideas. Include samples of your writing; even if you have no published articles to send, you can still send writing samples. Also include your résumé; editors are interested only in how your experience, training, and background pertain to what you are writing about.

HOOK THEM EARLY

The best query letters have a strong hook in the first two lines. What's a strong hook? Something that grabs the readers' attention and keeps them reading. In the past, all query letters were sent by "snail" mail, but today sending something by fax has been accepted by most editors, and online queries are becoming more acceptable. These more modern methods of communicating also give editors the chance to answer quickly without making you wait for weeks to hear. Sometimes a query may sit on a desk for a while, but be patient. You never know when a news-related story will prompt interest in your topic, no matter how obscure your profession.

THE STRUCTURE OF THE QUERY LETTER

Usually one to two single-spaced pages does the job. Whatever the length, most good queries are structured to include the editor's name and address,

---

Alex Haddox is a 36-year-old computer scientist and a member of the small, close-knit community of professional computer virus hunters, estimated at fewer than 100 people who are scattered around the world from Silicon Valley to Reykjavik, Iceland.

Alex wanted to reach the local business market outside the computer industry but didn't think he had anything interesting to say. We had Alex write a query letter to the editor explaining the history of computer viruses and what a virus hunter does when a new virus surfaces. We generated no interest until the White House, six months later, was attacked by a computer worm on July 19, 2001. Suddenly, the editor called back and wanted the story.

"A computer virus is a parasite," Alex's article began. "It will attach itself to a file, and every time the file is run the parasite runs first and takes control of the computer and then allows other files to run. As soon as all the files have run, the virus jumps on the files, piggybacks on them, and moves around from place to place like a worm. That's how it spreads."

the article's pitch, and your credentials. Many writers like to begin the query with a lead, perhaps the title of your article. Other writers start with a direct approach, giving some fact or information to hook the editor.

Even if you already know the subject well, it always pays to do some fresh research before you write the letter. Try to come up with a new statistic, something that may have been overlooked and shows the editor that you're bringing something new to the topic.

You want to close your letter by telling the editor how quickly you can deliver the piece. Monthly magazines are usually working two months ahead—in some cases, longer than that.

Your Credentials

If you have written articles for other magazines or been mentioned in other magazines, you want to include this information. Editors feel comfortable that you've delivered the goods for another magazine, especially one they've heard of.

An advanced degree in a field about which you're writing also helps convince the editor that you know how to write for that particular audience in a scholarly format.

If you haven't written any articles or have no credentials, there are still things you can do. One is to say nothing about your background and focus on the merits of the article. The other is to mention the number of years of experience you've had. You can also be honest and say it's the first article you've ever written.

Keep a file of the old query letters you've written and then go back to see which ones worked and which didn't.

Multi-Idea Queries

A lot of people recommend multiple queries, but I've found that simultaneous submitting is usually a bad idea. It's rather like asking someone to marry you but casually mentioning that you're talking to a few other candidates at the same time. If you don't mention in your query that you're sending out simultaneous submissions and other editors find out that you have, they feel they've been hoodwinked.

Don't send mass letters, photocopied letters, or anything else that doesn't look customized. Remember that an editor is a key part of your marketing plan, and you want to treat him as an important aspect of it. One article can make a career or reach tens of thousands of prospects.

What about just writing an article and sending it in? For a lot of trade magazine editors, that's just fine, especially a how-to piece because they assume they can always fix it up. But it's been my experience that it pays to inquire even though you've finished the article. Or include a query letter with the article, so the editor can quickly tell whether she's interested.

Next, *follow up*. Editors are busy, so you don't want to be a pest, but it's a matter of quietly pushing. First, make sure the editor receives your correspondence. I always send my work as priority mail. This says, "It's important." I also know I can call on the third day and ask, "Did you get my priority mail? I enclosed an article I authored that may be of value to your magazine." Then I shut up. I can hear the editor searching through her papers and, as she pulls mine out of the stack, say, "Yeah, I did, but I haven't gotten to it yet." The editor now has my piece in her hand and in the front of her mind. Then I wait for the response, which comes normally within a week but sometimes longer.

Here is a sample query letter to a newspaper editor:

Address

Dear Mr. Bob Jones,

"What Do You Do When the Stock Market Gets too High?" My lead is the best place for a beginning investor to get started in mutual funds. The article will cover how to find the mutual fund that's right for you, how to invest, and how to stay in the market for the long term. The article will be approximately 1,500 words long and can be completed in one week. I am willing to write the piece on spec. I have enclosed a copy of other reprints.

Warm regards,

Larry Chambers

A sample query letter to a magazine editor:

Ms. Rieva Lesonsky
Editor
Entrepreneur
2392 Morse Avenue
Irvine, CA 92614

Dear Ms. Lesonsky:

Traditionally, business owners have valued their companies based on their earnings and projections. What they are less familiar with is how to position their business strategically to maximize its value.

I'd like to submit the enclosed for your consideration as a feature article, which addresses how to enhance the worth of your business through assessing the company's competencies, identifying future opportunities, and poising the company to be ready for negotiating its sale. The article is entitled "Turbocharge Your Company's Value—The Three-Step Installation Guide."

Please contact me if you have any interest.

With kindest regards,

Larry Chambers

Enclosures

With commercial magazines, the wait can be as long as six to eight months. Trade magazines don't have large staffs or as much material coming in. They'll usually call back promptly and say, "I read your article. It sounds good, and I'd like to publish it in the next issue."

United Fresh Fruit and Vegetable Association

727 North Washington Street, Alexandria, Va. 22314

703/836-3410
Fax: 703/836-7745
Telex: 510 101-2401

July 31, 1989

Mr. Larry Chambers
Dean Witter Reynolds Inc.
800 Wilshire Boulevard
Los Angeles, CA 90017

Dear Mr. Chambers:

Sorry for the delay in getting back to you, but the news is good. Your article, "How To Successfully Manage Your Company Retirement Plan," is perfect for <u>Outlook</u> magazine. I am planning to run it in the next issue (dated July/August--we are running behind schedule). I'll make sure you get a few copies after it is published.

Thanks again for your contribution. Feel free to send me any other articles you think may be appropriate for our readers.

Sincerely,

Eric R. Wassyng
Director of Communications

11

What to Write

HOW TO CRAFT AN ARTICLE

I suggest using a problem/solution format for your article. This is probably the same basic structure of the presentation of your service or product when you talk with clients about their concerns. In the beginning of your article, point out the problem in one sentence, and tell readers that you're going to solve that problem. Next, explain the problem and its ramifications in more detail. Then explain how to avoid or resolve the problem. Tie it all together at the end. There's an old cliché in communications: *Tell them what you're going to tell them, tell them, and then tell them what you've told them.*

Stick with one subject. To give your writing focus, it's often helpful to distill the message in your own mind to a sentence or two.

The concept of writing like an expert has a logical starting point. You *are* the expert on what you know, so write from that point of view. When you know your business well, have thoroughly researched a topic, and can back up what you say, your writing voice will come across as the voice of authority. In fiction, a strong voice is created by tone and command of details. In nonfiction, a strong voice is created by tone and command of fact.

Readers respond to *showing*—not just telling. A good novel begins with a complication, which leads to developments—perhaps three, four, or five different ones—and then the resolution. The structure is similar in nonfiction; we start with the main problem, detail the effects of that problem, and then solve the problem.

When I first started, I simply wrote out all the problems my customers had and how we solved them. Suddenly, I was the expert on the subject, with the combined advice of all those specialists safely stored inside my notebook and tape recorder cassettes. All I needed was the organizational skills to transform my writing into a manuscript.

The way I write is the way I speak. I found this works best. I have worked with many organizations, and invariably they have an English major or a Ph.D. review my writing. Unless they are enrolled in, or understand, the credibility-marketing process, they go ballistic. They can't understand why the first draft looks so terrible.

Every year, hundreds of thousands of manuscripts, some totally grammatically correct, find the floor in the back office of a publishing concern. Time spent on correcting grammar means little if your article doesn't see the light of day. Your initial time should be spent on capturing ideas. Grammar is a process that originates on one side of the brain, while creativity comes from another. This could explain why so many English majors I've met have unpublished manuscripts and novels sitting under their *Roget's Thesaurus*.

Fragmented sentences can be favorable if they have an impact. Even single word sentences can be used if they grab the reader. Today's readers are victim's of information overload. In order to get published, your material must catch their attention in a very few words.

I love the story of novelist Pat Conroy arriving in New York to meet with his editor to finish *Beaches*. It is said that he carried in 2,000 hand-written pages, and the two spent the next six months sequestered in a room polishing and rewriting until they had a finished manuscript.

Think back to your college days or graduate programs, where you were bombarded with professional narratives. Week after week, you were assigned lengthy books for argument and analysis. They were not intended to enlighten or move readers but focused largely on engaging you to challenge what other professionals have already said.

What makes for good reading is unraveling problems or revealing new information, not abstract debates. When Stephen Hawking wrote *A Brief History of Time,* he was told by his publisher that for every formula he added to his books, he'd lose 10,000 readers.

Keep in mind why you are writing: to build your visibility and credibility. To do this, you need to write something that can be understood. Be willing to experiment and you'll find the rewards for your efforts are greater visibility.

PLAN YOUR STORY: EIGHT RECOMMENDATIONS

1. Identify the main premise you want the reader to learn. Use that point as the working title. Most first-time writers spend a lot of time picking out the perfect title. But selecting a title is the least important aspect of writing and placing your article because most editors change the title when the article is published. I normally don't title an article until I've written the entire thing and then find the title somewhere in the manuscript.

2. When preparing your articles, write them as though you were speaking to a friend about your product or service. It can start with an anecdote—as I do in a lot of these chapters. An anecdote is popular with how-to pieces. It can be a little story about someone who experienced what the article is going to discuss. This strategy also keeps them reading for the solution. That hooks the target reader in a real and personal way—and you've done it in the first sentence!

3. Try to find some compelling research or data your reader hasn't heard or seen yet that supports your point. Published articles that educate, solve a problem, or convey a successful or advantageous situation can be even more effective than client referrals in generating new business. Success sells success—and highly educated professionals are always looking for timely information that will increase their wealth. Business readers are much more likely to respond favorably to a solution to a problem from someone who communicates expertise than from someone who is boasting about his firm. *Write to educate.*

4. Make your article concise and to the point, concentrating on getting all the facts. Trade magazine stories seek articles that show readers how to save money and time and improve their life. Trade journal readers are very busy people. They read, not for entertainment, but for information that can help them. Be specific. Introduce a particular problem and describe its solution and results, or discuss the latest development in the industry and reasons for it; and, finally, organize the structure so it's easy for the reader to understand and follow.

5. Support your claims and statements with statistical examples, studies, or explanations. Double-check your facts. If in doubt, make sure. Be thorough. People who read your articles may make decisions or procedural changes based on what you've written. They require accurate and complete information. Keep your notes and source materials for at least six months after the article has been published.

6. Be objective. Your article should contain useful, accurate, and honest information and advice, not rewritten corporate bulletins and press releases. If you do a story on money management, talk to several different money managers, not just one. If you're giving a new management perspective, give the pros as well as the cons. One-sidedness doesn't interest editors. They want the disadvantages, as well as the advantages, spelled out. Don't write about yourself. Don't write advertisements. An editor will see through such an obvious ploy and the article won't get past his desk.

7. Never write about something that will be out of date within a few weeks. Sometimes it takes three, four, or up to six months before your article may appear. Write in a timeless style. A timeless subject is not dependent on current events, the market, or a particular stock price. A timeless article is as relevant and marketable three years from now as it was the day it was written.

8. Most important, make sure your solution answers the problem or point you stated at the beginning. Figure 11.1 diagrams the structure of an article for publication, including the major issues to be addressed.

Now it's time for the payoff, when your planning, thinking, and organizing begin to take a more satisfying shape. It's time for you to write your first full draft. You shouldn't feel too uneasy about it now because everything's in

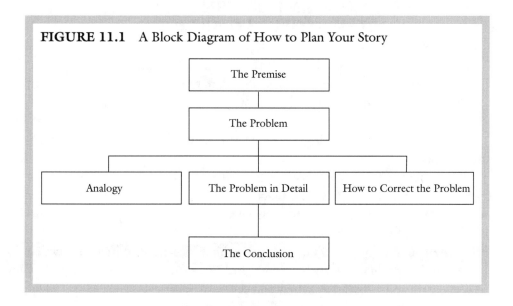

FIGURE 11.1 A Block Diagram of How to Plan Your Story

The Premise

The Problem

Analogy | The Problem in Detail | How to Correct the Problem

The Conclusion

place, but it's natural that you want to delay the challenge of committing words to paper. But if you've done the preparation that I've suggested, it's time for action.

WHAT IF YOU'VE NEVER WRITTEN BEFORE?

Here's my contention: If you can tell an interesting tale, you can write an interesting story. Most everyone I've met who's been in business for any length of time is used to telling stories to explain their services or sell a product. It is my belief that writing is just speech frozen on paper with the advantage of a little editing.

What if you don't have time? Don't worry; you don't have to spend a lot of time doing this. In my workshop, we've got this down to a seven-minute process!

If you follow the following steps, I guarantee you can produce a complete story. And it will be your story. There are no hypothetical examples here to copy. You can use this blueprint many times, creating a variety of how-to articles. Work at your own pace and your own level, and as you improve, challenge yourself. But first you're going to need a pen and paper. So let's begin!

THE CARD GAME: SEVEN EASY STEPS TO WRITING AN ARTICLE

Number a set of index cards and jot the following information on the cards. This way, you can spot inconsistencies or change the content before you begin to write. You can also move the cards around and play with them.

Card 1. Jot down the single biggest problem affecting your customers and/or clients.

I'll have Jerry Dipoto demonstrate this with you. Jerry is the president of a trust company that buys financial practices. He told me a major problem for many of his clients is that they don't have an exit strategy when they plan to sell their business.

On the backside of the same card, pose this problem as a question, which will set up the rest of your article. Jerry's problem posed as a question is "How do you create an exit strategy when you sell your business?"

Card 2. Identify three related problems that are a result of the main problem. For example:

1. The business isn't prepared to be sold.
2. Sellers don't know how to determine the worth of their business.
3. Buyers want the sellers to sign an employment contract.

Now write your problems.

Card 3. Here is where you show us what you know. Solve the problem! Provide steps or actions to correct the main problem. This is not intended to pitch your service or product but to provide readers with the answer or alternatives to the problem(s) you described. It could include a series of steps and is the reason readers continue reading your article.

Card 4. Write down any relevant discoveries or recent developments that readers wouldn't likely have heard yet. Set aside charts and evidence. You don't have to be the originator of new information; quotations and excerpts indicate that you have your finger on the pulse of the industry. Provide evidence or an outside reference that will offer objective proof and support such as findings from research studies. Include relevant charts and/or graphs. Some of this information may require permission to use. Be sure to name the source.

Card 5. Write a short personal story that can be used to illustrate the problem. This is my favorite and, I believe, the reason why my clients have been able to get published by major publishers. A personal story establishes a strong initial connection with those readers who can relate to the experience. At its simplest, you grab readers' attention by relating a pertinent thought, insight, or observation that gets your main point across. Don't be afraid to write down what you see, smell, and hear. This will set up time and place.

Mary Harris gets the prize for this one. Last month we did this exercise in a seminar she attended, and I asked for a volunteer to tell a personal experience. Mary got up and started telling us a delightful story about an experience when she was 11 years old:

> I had this great idea to save my baby-sitting money. I got a large
> balloon [her goal was to fill it] and covered it with strips of newspaper

dipped in a paste of flour and water. Then I painted the papier-mâché balloon beautiful colors.

Every time I got a dollar from baby sitting, I'd drop it in the slit in the top of the balloon bank. Finally, it was the last day of summer, and I calculated I had enough money to buy school clothes. So I held a big celebration and cut open the papier-mâché balloon with a knife. At first I thought I'd been robbed. All the dollars had somehow interacted with the paste, which never completely dried inside, so all the dollars I'd saved all summer long had turned to soup.

Everyone loved her story. "You'd better know what's going on inside your 401(k) plan so you don't cut it open at retirement and find your dollars have turned to soup!" was the caption we used.

Now move your personal experience to the opening of your article.

Card 6. This is a call to action, a simple thing that can make a big difference. It could be an invitation, such as "Contact the author for more information," or a self-test or worksheet.

Card 7. Conclude with information your reader can use in a summary. The more clearly and forcefully stated, the greater the likelihood that what you say will be remembered accurately. The conclusion could be another personal experience or anecdote, this time with a positive outcome that portrays an opportunity. Or it could be a "quick-start" list, something like "Five things you can do to . . ."

Now read your cards out loud. Don't worry if it's not perfect. For now you just want to make sure you have everything in place. Does the ending answer the question you posed at the beginning? That's the built-in test.

Congratulations! This creates the basic outline, the architecture of your article, the framework of the house, so to speak—and it probably took less than seven minutes to do. If the article's for a newspaper, it should be no longer than 750 words; if it's for a magazine, it should be no longer than 1,500 words, about seven or eight double-spaced typed pages. And you probably already have three of those pages in notes. Now all you have to do is flesh out each point.

Most important, you now know what you have to say. This may prove to be a self-enlightening experience that increases your awareness of all aspects of your market, clarifies your stance or beliefs, and/or affirms and validates what you have to offer.

I'm too busy, you say. Okay, continue your normal work routine but write a little each day if possible—even if it's only a handful of words or a paragraph. The cards will help you restart where you left off. In fact, you have an advantage over most other writers, who are not as well organized. You have your story starters, which is your analogy and your opening sentence. Keep looking at your cards that describe the story problem, the article problem, and the article-ending answer to the question. That will keep you on track. Refer to your cards often as you move along.

Follow the card steps consistently. Stay with your sequence of cards or the block diagram or both. Both should be neatly identified, although the cards will provide more detail. Abandoning your cards in some burst of inspiration may send you off course, and you'll find yourself writing an entirely different article a few pages down the line. If that happens and you start rambling, look at the cards and just say to yourself, "What's the point of the article?" And that'll get you back on track.

This is your first draft; give it a once-over with this final checklist in mind:

- What is your article about?
- What is your question or problem?
- Does it appear early in your story?
- Does your story focus on your article problem or question?
- How many steps are in your article?
- Does each step lead logically to the next step and so on?
- Does each step open with a clearly stated or understood goal of that paragraph?
- Compare your story with your planning blocks or cards. Have you left anything out?
- Did you contrive an ending that leaves the reader feeling they've learned something?
- Does the end answer the question that you posed at the beginning?
- Did you edit your article for grammar and spelling?
- Is your manuscript neat, on good quality bond paper with clear typing and one-inch margins?

As you review this first draft, I suggest you keep in mind that what this is, is a first, or working, draft.

THE REWRITE

Ideally, you should leave yourself enough time to put the draft aside so that you can forget at least some of what you were thinking when you first wrote it. The very worst time to revise a draft is right after you have finished it. At that moment you are the worst possible editor. You know too much about what you have written and are, thereby, constitutionally incapacitated from reading your essay objectively.

A group of researchers at Carnegie-Mellon University created a passage on a technical subject and inserted into it problems of organization, sentence structure, clarity, and the like. They asked two groups of readers to read the passage and indicate where they had trouble understanding. One group, however, was given background reading in the subject of the passage before they read it. Which group was better able to identify those deliberately inserted problems?

The readers *without* the background reading, of course! When the ones with the better knowledge hit a passage with errors, they were able to bring up from memory what they already knew. They didn't spot the errors in the writing because they were not relying on the writing to understand the ideas—they already understood. The ones without previous knowledge were much more effective at spotting flaws because they were much more attentive to the text. Without the background reading, the only way they could understand the material was to concentrate on the text.

When you reread your own writing, you aren't really reading it; you're only reminding yourself of what you intended to say when you wrote it. That means the longer you can set aside something you have written before you revise it, the more you will have forgotten what you were thinking when you wrote it.

Remember, keep it simple. This is the quality of straightforwardness. Stick to the most interesting highlights. Be thorough. Readers may make decisions based on your advice. Make sure your facts are correct and every quotation is accurate. Don't wax poetic or try to impress the reader with your thesaurus. Einstein managed to sum up the entire universe in a single sentence. Industry-specific jargon should be explained or not used at all. Use common, everyday language that people can relate to and everybody can identify with. Surprisingly, awkwardness or an ingenuous lack of perfection is endearing to a reader, and most successful writers have discovered this. As you write and rewrite, you are unconsciously absorbing and picking up your own rhythm and phrasing, finding your writing voice.

Now you polish.

Polishing

The final level of writing is the polished level. The process of polishing is concerned with grammar, word usage, and various principles of sentence and paragraph structure. Because this is the only level of composition that the reader ever sees directly, most people have no idea how many rewrites and corrections have to be made from the original draft. Don't worry if everything isn't perfect. Most of us weren't English majors, and that's okay. That's not our expertise. Editors will clean up your work if you've got good material.

YOUR BIO

Now here's where you can promote yourself! Include your bio and a short statement about who you are, what you do, and a phone number and address. You can make it fun. In my case, a producer for the History Channel was at his editor's home in Ojai reading my book about my Ranger experience. When he got to the last page of the book and read that "Larry Chambers now resides in Ojai, California," he phoned me. We met and I was hired as a technical advisor for the program about my book.

TITLES

Writers often make the mistake of putting a lot of energy into getting the title right. Don't get too attached to your article's title. It's probably going to get changed. Headlines almost always get changed. The text could also go through a change. Depending on the magazine and your article, it may change a little or a lot. Just make sure your message still comes across when an editor is through with it.

When people are under pressure, amusing mistakes can happen. The following are actual titles that slipped past an editor:

- Astronaut Takes Blame for Gas in Spacecraft
- Something Went Wrong in Jet Crash, Expert Says
- Include Your Children When Baking Cookies
- Miners Refuse to Work after Death
- Clinton Wins on Budget; But More Lies Ahead
- War Dims Hope for Peace

- Police Begin Campaign to Run Down Jaywalkers
- Panda Mating Fails; Veterinarian Takes Over
- Typhoon Rips Through Cemetery; Hundreds Dead
- If Strike Isn't Settled Quickly, It May Last Awhile
- New Study of Obesity Looks for Larger Test Group

HOW TO CLONE YOUR WORK, OR REPACKAGING THE SAME MATERIAL FOR A DIFFERENT AUDIENCE

Usually this means keeping the basic concept the same but taking a different slant or approach. Because trade magazines aren't like mainstream commercial magazines, there isn't necessarily a conflict of interest in writing the same article for various trades. Most ideas lend themselves to at least several variations and can potentially spawn many alternate approaches and/or points of view for a variety of intended target audiences.

For example, one of our articles was published in *Ocular Surgery News* targeting doctors concerned about their retirement plans. The article explained how to find a money manager and the best ways to manage funds in the stock market. Aside from *Ocular Surgery News,* a logical market for this article would be medical journals or various magazines that not only offer medical advice but also have a financial news slant. With a minor rewrite, this article might be appropriate for small business owners or maybe contractors, who have the same problems with managing money.

One money manager built a multihundred-million-dollar business using public relations and magazine reprints as his marketing tools. In fact, he has repackaged one investment article over 20 times in different versions. He takes an article specifically written for small business owners, for example, and replaces any references to small business owners with the word *physicians* or another professional group.

Notice, by the way, that each of these target groups read noncompeting publications. Each has its own unique readership and its own needs, concerns, and expectations. Your networked article must match its intended audience. Treat each rewrite as a new unpublished piece. If, however, it has only a few minor changes and is largely identical to the piece you've already had published, then you must treat it as a reprint.

When approaching additional publications, following are some etiquette tips to remember:

- Mention in your cover letter to the editor where your work on the same topic has already been published or is scheduled to be published. This also demonstrates that you can write a publishable piece.
- Don't sell the same piece or a similar piece to publications with overlapping readerships. In other words, you wouldn't want to try to sell an article to competing magazines because many of the same people read both magazines.
- You may submit the same article to as many different publications at a time as you like—making sure they do not have overlapping readerships. Newspapers work on a very tight schedule and, occasionally, rushed freelance material gets into print with the paper neglecting to inform the author until the day of publication or even a day after, which could lead to two newspapers with similar readership publishing your same article.

FOLLOW-UP ARTICLES THAT GET RESULTS

Write an article based on a theme or premise, such as ten ways to save money in health care. The follow-up could be ten *more* healthy ways to save money. The only drawback in writing a follow-up is that it often takes as much time and effort as writing the original article. An unusually long article could be broken into a multiple-part series. A popular theme could become a monthly column.

Because you've written one article, editors think of you as an expert. When they need articles written, they contact you. If you've worked with an editor once, he will certainly be willing to consider your next submission. That's how contributing authors get started. As you continue to move up the ladder, your articles could lead to radio and TV interviews. Media programmers are always looking for a recognizable expert to fill out and add credible material to an interview.

Now use everything you just learned when you write copy for your ads, newsletters, and Web sites.

A KILLER AD

A friend of mine in Ojai has a villa in Tuscany. It's an amazing place with a medieval garden, a pool, tennis courts, library, and a cellar that had been converted to a movie room. It was actually a restored 100-year-old farmhouse with heavy wooden doors and thick stone walls. To get there, you drive past a vineyard up a winding country road past thick hedges ripe with blackberries. And to top it off, it's silhouetted by the Tuscany hills.

My friend couldn't understand why he was getting little results running stiff formal ads in the back of travel magazines. "100-year-old villa for rent in Tuscany." So many people like my friend think the solution to marketing is where you place the ad. But spending time thinking about what you want to say can go a long way to success. We visited his place last summer and helped him write a short article about the place. We played with the language and got creative.

The article started with us standing in the kitchen: "It smelled like fresh bread. The kitchen had ten-foot-high plastered ceilings and the shelves were lined with glass containers. Even the humming of the old refrigerator sounded Italian." Then we had him describe the villa: How it was only 12 miles south-east of Florence and a mile from the small village of Tori; and how the villa came with a cook, a maid, and two groundskeepers. He had over 20 queries from the following issue.

A MULTI-MILLION-DOLLAR ARTICLE

When John Bowen was CEO of RWB, an asset management company located in Silicon Valley, he wrote an article about the way he managed his business. His goal was to build credibility for his firm. He had no idea that six months after the article appeared, he'd get a phone call that would increase the value of his company by millions, but his article did just that!

The article was published in an obscure trade magazine that his industry reads. A subscriber put it in his desk until six months later, when he remembered a friend who was interested in making a business move. He sent his friend the dog-eared article. Because the article resonated with his personal beliefs, the friend contacted the author. Three months later he moved more than $63 million of recurring business to John Bowen's company.

Can you imagine handing one of your clients an article you wrote that explained how your business works and how you help your clients. When you follow this strategy, it can be more rewarding than you ever hoped!

MOMENTUM

Selective Exposure

Your Message

Your Prospect

12

Media Play

If the idea of appearing on television or being interviewed on the radio or Internet puts you off for any reason, here is a little insight into how to overcome your concerns that leaves you free to be the expert and create unforgettable interviews and presentations.

Let's say you found a publisher after writing a book, and one of the producers from the Oprah Winfrey show called to ask you to appear on the show and talk about your book. What are you going to do then?

A psychologist told me, "When I teach my class, I talk off the top of my head to 200 people for three hours with no break. Just before I take the podium, I take a deep breath and surrender. I tell myself, 'I'm going to do the best I can and if they like it, great, and if they don't like it, oh well. I just won't have to answer as many questions afterward.' That makes me smile, and I walk out in front of my audience relaxed."

Some time ago, I was on a commercial airline flight to Amsterdam. We had just flown over Philadelphia, when the captain announced that it might get a little rough and told us to fasten our safety belts. That was the last we heard from him, as the cabin lights began to flicker. I looked out my window and watched the tip of the wing disappear in the clouds, and we began losing altitude. There was a lot of commotion and noise, and the woman in the seat next to me grabbed my arm and screamed in my ear, "Are we going to die?"

It felt as if the plane was bouncing in place. My tray table dropped open and I grabbed it and held on, as I pressed my face against the window. Adrenalin was pumping in my chest and I felt as though I couldn't breathe. Then the plane bounced harder and fell suddenly. It felt like it fell a thousand feet before the pilot got it leveled out. The flight smoothed out; but for the next six hours, I stayed watching against the window, trying to anticipate each bounce and bump and praying they'd stop. When we landed, I was the last one off the plane and walked out with the pilots. I wanted to know why he never came back on the speaker to tell us it was going to be okay. He looked tired and told me we had been hit by lightning, and he had been too terrified to speak!

That's about the level of stress I used to feel when I first walked up in front of a group to make a presentation. Several years ago, I even invested $3,000 for a weeklong workshop to learn how to present myself in the best light. The workshop, with 100 participants and 3 instructors, was held at a remote retreat in northern California. For the first couple of days, we were each videotaped giving our best ten-minute presentation to the entire group; and we repeated this at the end of the course. At the end of each presentation, everyone in the audience scored the speaker by holding up one of the cards numbered from one, for the lowest, to ten, for the highest.

I was nervous but had made a lot of presentations to clients. So I figured I'd probably get only sevens the first go-around; then, by the end of the course, I'd make my way up to some nines and tens. I'd be the best in the class; people would come up and say, "Larry, how did you do it? We've seen business presentations, and . . . well . . . could you come back to the school and be one of the instructors?" But, of course, that's not what happened.

I came out dressed in my best power suit—dark blue pinstripe with a yellow tie and white shirt. I gave my talk and then watched as the cards went up. They were almost all the same—ones and twos! All 99 people said I stunk—I was floored. In fact, I argued with one of the instructors and wanted to leave the course. This instructor asked me to just sit down and think about it. He promised I would feel different by the end of the week.

Well, I stayed and continued to participate, but I couldn't really understand much of what was being taught. At the end of the week, my scores improved to fours. Because the presentations were on videotape, I watched myself. It was painful, but what did I care? The course was over.

Not long afterward, I received an invitation from my employer, EF Hutton, to its national sales conference, not just as a participant but as the keynote speaker, because I had opened up more new accounts that year than anyone in our firm. I had just finished the speaking class, so I wouldn't have to prepare anything; I could wing it. The participants wanted to hear some "secret" about how I had been able to open so many accounts. There wasn't any secret, so I thought I'd try to make it funny.

After a great introduction, I walked up to the stage and looked out at my peers. I told them how I'd trick or convince a receptionist or secretary to interrupt some executive, and when I got him on the phone, I'd begin my sales pitch with an "assumed close." At appointments, I'd maneuver a way to sit in my prospect's chair to reduce his power. Once, I even let my pen drop into the prospect's hands so I could get him to sign the contract I was holding.

"Hit them hard and fast," I said. "And spend the rest of the time finding out where they have their other assets." Then I pantomimed grabbing my prospect, holding him upside down, and shaking him until every cent in his pocket was on the ground. "I put prospects in the highest payoff products we offer," I continued; and I concluded, "And that is why I keep picking up the phone day after day to make more cold calls."

There was dead silence; everyone just sat in shock. No one moved as if they were embarrassed. They had expected to hear something inspirational—not conspiratorial. They wanted to feel enlightened—not exposed. But what did I know? I just wanted to be liked and make them laugh. Rather than trying to impart useful information, I was trying to control the response. I didn't talk about how I dealt with rejection, or how many times I would follow up before I gave up on a prospect, or how afraid I was of not making my numbers next month.

I have a friend who's a true perfectionist. He's very controlling and can't allow himself to fail. He won't take risks or compete where he's not assured of winning. The fear of being seen as a failure stops him from many pursuits.

If you want to be highly visible, maybe on television, you have to be able to get up in front of people and speak naturally and in the audience's language. The secret is to be real and focused on the needs and concerns of your audience, not yourself.

Recently, I was interviewed for a History Channel program. The other interviewees took it very seriously; some even used it as a forum to make a political statement. At the last minute before I went on camera, I put on my Hawaiian shirt and said, "Let's have fun." I was very relaxed and the producer ended up using most of my interview in the show.

Why did that work? I wasn't focused on myself. I was there primarily as a technical advisor, making sure the other participants were okay. So when it was my turn to go in front of the camera, I wasn't anxious about how I would look or sound. In the past, I would have been in an anxiety trance—totally concerned about everyone's judging me!

When you go into the anxiety trance, your conscious mind goes bye-bye. Your thought processes become gridlocked; you can't remember names, dates, and other details. You get embarrassed, your face gets hot, you start to sweat, your stomach becomes upset, and you have a "shame attack." Anyone who tells you it's easy to get up in front of a camera or do a seminar must be a professional; it's rated one of the top stress-related activities in our society.

When I started being paid to make seminar presentations, I wanted to be sure to give participants their money's worth, so I enrolled in a stand-up comedy course. I never realized how hard it is to be funny. I wasn't funny. I wasn't even interesting.

After a couple of humiliating attempts, our instructor could see I was winging it. I didn't have any material. Standing in front of a group is like swimming; you can't fake it, and you either swim . . . or sink. Everyone in the class had polished and polished. It forced me to practice, rehearse, and really know my subject.

I also learned something else: When I addressed a group of people, I was too busy watching their reactions. If just one person seemed uninterested, I would go brain dead and forget my place. I wanted to do something or say something that could help me get over that. The coaching for this was to simply select someone in the audience with whom to make a connection by commenting on what I saw. I tried it in the comedy class and got a big laugh (my first one). I immediately relaxed back into my material as if I were speaking to some old friends.

Soon afterward, I was in Dallas to speak to over 300 people just before the meal break. Usually, I'd be shaking, worrying about keeping that many people interested. But this time, I took a deep breath, assured in the fact that I really knew my material. After my introduction, I walked up to the podium, looked out at the crowd, and said, "This crowd looks hungry," and everyone started laughing. I couldn't believe it. I hadn't planned that, but it took the pressure off, got me started, and everyone said they got a lot out of what I had to say.

You become authentic when you stop trying to control what you can't control. For example, I've learned I can't control getting published, but I can control how good the article is, where I choose to submit it, and how I write the query letter. I do have control over what goes into my writing.

The real source of my power is having a process that feeds and nourishes me and makes me feel good about myself. For me, the process is writing and speaking. Staying in the process allows me to detach. When I'm detached, I could stand in front of the world.

It's my belief that writing articles and/or books is not just for the obvious marketing reasons. The real reason you need to write is that, in the process of doing it, you become an expert in your field. You'll have to research things you haven't thought about and be able to put them down in writing. It builds your conviction. The more you write, the more you become an expert and the more that's going to come through when you speak to prospects. People pick up on your authenticity.

The world is hungry for real people—authentic and honest. Being real allows you to enter into your prospect's model of the world. I tell prospective writers that they have to know their business so well that they can present it, write about it, and talk to clients about it in understandable terms—understandable from the clients' perspective. They're more likely to listen to you when you speak their language.

13

An Unforgettable Presentation

The golden award for the best live sales presentation goes to Amway's Diamond Direct from Atlanta, Georgia—Coleman Orr! I saw him at the Dallas Hyatt Regency, along with 10,000 screaming followers. Inside the grand ballroom, rows and rows of chairs were lined up concert style facing a huge raised podium. Two men were testing the sound system, while a guard stood at the back by the door. "Check. Check."

The stage resembled a mini version of the Academy Awards. I knew the Amway distributors liked to flaunt expensive cars, furs, and diamonds, but this was outrageous. On the stage was a new Cadillac, a showcase full of jewelry, and an armed security guard standing behind a long table covered with fur coats. In one corner of the room was a grand piano.

Suddenly, the theme song from *Rocky* swelled the room. Coleman came out and stood at the center of the stage. Hundreds of people started jumping, shouting, and tossing confetti. The music seemed even louder and balloons were flying and popping everywhere.

"I sell soap," he started when the noise died down. "They laughed at me and they'll laugh at you. A...m...w...a...y," he said slowly, spelling each letter out. "A...m...w...a...y. You're going to get a little of it. Man, I tell you, we got three kids; the oldest one's crying 'cause his teeth are falling out, the youngest one's cryin' 'cause his teeth are comin' in; the kid in the middle will bite you in the leg. Okay? You ain't no different." The crowd roared even louder this time.

"I checked into a hotel last week; they said, 'Oh, yeah, you're with Amway.' I said, 'I ain't with Amway, mister, you're looking at a half a billion dollars in the flesh—I'm living it; my momma's in it; my daddy's in it; my brother's in it; my sister's in it; my wife's friends are in it—I got A's in my blood! A-M-W-A-Y!'"

The room felt electric. I'd heard about legendary "southern revivals," but I'd never experienced anything like this. I turned around and saw rows of ordinary-looking people jumping out of their seats or sitting frozen, listening raptly to every word that Coleman uttered. He bent down on one knee. "You say you want the world, yet you hesitate." He stopped, his hands stretched out.

"Nobody gonna steal my dream, people. They try to steal it from me—they been stealing yours all your life—you'll go outside that door on Wednesday, Thursday, Friday—you're gonna call somebody up and say, 'I'd like you to come over and see something.' And they're gonna say, 'What is it?' Say, 'Man, it don't matter if I'm shoveling manure. I'm inviting you and your wife over to have a cup of coffee with my wife and me. And if you're too good to come, let me know now.'"

He slowly fanned his arm in a wide arch while his eyes connected with everyone in the room. "There are millions upon millions of people out there looking for what we've got. And we've got it right here. In this room." The room vibrated with wild applause.

He was just selling soap. A simple product you can buy off the shelf. But not to these people. Not tonight. It was a way to make payments on the farm or fix a fence. Buy a new car instead of a set of jumper cables. And they looked at Coleman the way people must have watched Babe Ruth before he hit a home run over the right field fence. I felt it too, caught up in the ocean of frenzy in the room. He was magnificent.

What Coleman did that put people into such a trance was to talk in huge and abstract terms. He'd make nouns into a process. He'd begin speaking about things like truth and beauty and honor—and you have to go inside your head and figure out what that means for you. Abstract concepts have no objective reference but exist only in name. What these abstracts mean for you are probably different than what they mean to me. In psychology, this is also called the "Milton" model, after Milton Eriksen.

If you tell a different type of story, say one about getting the jack out of the trunk, jacking up the back of the car, taking out the lug wrench, and then loosening the lug nuts, you're using some very specifically defined language. There's not much doubt about what you're talking about, so the listener can stay present. We don't have to go into a trance generally to talk about changing a tire.

But the more Coleman uses his kinds of words, nominalizations, and speaks in long run-on sentences, I get so hypnotized that my head is spinning. He'd give one of his one-hour speeches, and you clap and scream, "Yeah, that sounds great." And if someone asked you later on, "What did that guy talk to you about?" you'll say, "I don't know, but it was a great speech."

RECOMMENDATIONS FOR MAKING MEMORABLE PRESENTATIONS

In the business world today, the ability to excel in making oral presentations is a definite requirement for advancement. You may never care to speak like Coleman, but my point is that he speaks from the heart. You could feel his words.

The following is a simple eight-step presentation plan that can help you get your point across and ensure success at your next meeting:

1. Plan what you are going to say.
2. Know your audience.
3. Pull your audience in with a strong attention statement.
4. State what it is you are going to say. Say it, then tell your audience what you said.
5. Anticipate any questions.
6. Make your points again while answering questions.
7. Use visual aids.
8. Speak from conviction and the heart.

Conceptually, a presentation is divided into three sections: the beginning, the middle, and the end. This simple structure will keep you on course.

The Beginning Section of a Presentation

First, state your point, conclusion, recommendation, and action plan. You'll be surprised how many presenters never really state their point to the audience. You need to formulate your message so it is absolutely clear to the audience what it is you want them to do.

The function of your opening is to clearly state your message, outline supporting arguments, and prepare listeners for the detailed discussion that follows the presentation. The opening has another function as well. Besides introducing your message, the opening is your chance to get your listeners' attention.

Grab their attention. Attention is a prerequisite to communication. The more of the audience's attention you have, the more communicating you can do. Using an introduction that captures your listeners' attention is a necessity. Coleman used personal stories to pull in his audience. An audience is like a Missouri mule—you can reason with it, but you first have to hit it over the head to get its attention. You want not merely to capture your listeners' attention but to engage their minds, and nothing engages a group like speaking from the heart. We call this kind of attention-getting kickoff "the grabber."

The lead. The lead should introduce the topic in a catchy, arresting, or amusing manner. It should also serve to introduce you, creating a connection between you and your listeners. At its simplest, you need to grab your listeners' attention relating to a pertinent thought, insight, or observation that gets your point across.

The Middle Section of a Presentation

The presentation's middle is its guts. It's where the information is imparted and the persuasion takes place. Without good, hard information in the middle, all the audience profiling and message tailoring in the world isn't going to mean much. Don't fall into the trap of putting all your time and effort into the ending and beginning but leaving the middle to take care of itself.

There are three basic formats you can use to structure the middle of a presentation. They are:

1. Question and answer (Q&A)
2. Topical
3. Problem/solution

Question and answer. The Q&A approach analyzes a problem or task and puts it into a series of questions requiring answers. For example, a question needing exploration in a marketing plan might be: What type of media support do we have?

Topical. This format says, "Here are the topics that need to be dealt with and resolved in a particular situation."

Problem/Solution. This scenario works well for reporting results. It usually goes something like this: "As you know, we've been facing a serious and unanticipated cash-flow problem, stemming ultimately from a troublesome deterioration in accounts receivable."

In other words, the problem/solution format involves a concise statement detailing the elements of the problem, followed by an outline of how solutions were developed. This leads to a detailed discussion of the significant stages and findings. If there are many facts in the middle of your presentation, it is a good idea to summarize your progress from time to time.

List the selling points. List the selling points supporting your conclusion. Very often, a strong selling point makes an excellent grabber. Especially effective selling points are those that stimulate the intellect, provoke a "gee-whiz" response, appeal to a sense of self-interest or well-being, or touch an emotional button or the pocketbook. Here is where you use supporting data, statistics, research findings, and other proof.

Visual aids. The typical listener forgets 40 percent of what he or she has heard in the first half hour, 60 percent by the end of the day, and 90 percent after a week. Every accomplished presenter knows that using visual aids increases retention. These aids can consist of overhead transparencies, color slides, videotapes, or, in the case of General Schwarzkopf, large color charts. A visual aid helps in making your point, a point your audience will remember. A study by the 3M Corporation and the University of Minnesota, which was conducted to update a similar study by The Wharton School of the University of Pennsylvania, found that an audience is 43 percent more likely to be persuaded by the use of visual aids.

The Ending Section of a Presentation

You've told 'em what you were gonna tell 'em and you've told 'em. Now it simply remains to tell 'em what you told 'em and to drive it home to 'em.

The ending should take no more than one minute. The reasoning here is the same as for the beginning: The talk's end is the last thing your audience will hear, and the last thing heard is the thing most likely remembered. The more clearly and forcefully it is stated, the greater the likelihood that it will be remembered accurately.

A SAMPLE SPEECH

Don't hurry into this. There is a high liability when you speak; you set yourself up to be judged. I was invited to speak at my former Army Ranger Unit's Annual Awards Ball. I used an outline to organize my thoughts. I've included it here as it may help next time you have to prepare for a talk.

I started with a call for the audience's help.

I'm going to need your help. I'm not a professional speaker, but I've been asked to talk about the history of the 101st Airborne L Co 75th Rangers and what that unit means to me. Well, I would love to tell you about my very first days in the unit, how we went through a tough selection process and combat, but before I tell you my story, what about yours?

Can you remember back? What happened to you? How did it make you feel?

(PAUSE)

I can tell you I had a great sense of pride. I didn't know what I was getting myself into. I volunteered and, you know what, everyone else sittin' in that tent thought I was crazy, and maybe at that point I was, but on some level I knew that what I was about to do would make a real difference in my life. It foreshadowed what was to come.

(PAUSE)

I established my credibility:

After I was selected, I went through the training. Well, I don't know how you felt about your training, but I had some pretty strong feelings about it. My favorite part was after it was over. The greatest experience I ever had, though, was with the people I served with. And the bonds that were formed have lasted 30 years. I'd like to share a couple of stories with you and, as I share these stories, I want you to think of your buddies.

[Include a couple of anecdotes.]

I finished by motivating them:

1. Perseverance. Never quit. It's never over until it's over.
2. Confidence. Be confident going into every situation.
3. Courage. That doesn't mean not being afraid. It means trusting in your abilities.
4. Pride. Be proud of what you do every day of your life. Stand for something you can be proud of. It's okay to be a little cocky; remember you will always be a Ranger.

SUMMARY

In preparing an oral presentation, these four rules should prove helpful:

1. Write your conclusion first.
2. List supporting material—that is, your selling points: data, facts, statistics, research, examples.
3. Find an appropriate grabber.
4. The ending should contain two elements: a summary of key points and a call for action.

14

A Great Interview

Okay, you've worked on your presentation. You've done seminars and workshops. You're ready to take your presentation to the media.

Let's say somebody from a local print medium or television station contacts you for an interview. Are you prepared to speak? Remember that the media are looking first at their own needs, and their biggest need is to provide stimulating television or controversial radio or an exciting article or feature. Remember, too, that journalism thrives on sensationalism. Don't assume to know up front why you're being contacted.

Many people who participate in different media events are unwilling to adapt their style to fit the media's needs. As a result, they're ineffective in getting their message across. Your specific goal is to showcase yourself in the best light.

When I first started to deal with the press, I soon discovered that you have to be careful and specific; and you can't assume that the press understands what you're saying. You have to be literal with the written press; otherwise, reporters write what they *think* they heard you say.

It's very common for TV talk show guests to be folksy and try to banter with the host. Don't try to be a comedian or an entertainer—that's the job of the host. While TV hosts are relaxed and conversational, they are also careful to maintain their professional credibility.

Work on a presentation that simplifies a complex subject like economics for the layperson. Economic concepts are actually very logical—what confuses people is the jargon of the discipline. Before your talk, take a moment or two to consider what you want to say to your audience. What is it that you are offering? Do you have charts or quotations you can use to support the claims that you are going to make?

WHAT DO YOU DO WHEN A REPORTER CALLS?

Start by asking the reason for the call. If you're caught off guard, ask if you can call back. This allows you time to prepare your answers. Keep the reporter interested; give her a reason to continue the conversation. Make sure she knows you've done your homework and that you have something of importance to offer her audience.

Reporters are always in a hurry, always up against a deadline. They may be young and inexperienced and don't know where to get information, yet even experienced reporters need you in critical ways. A reporter is not the expert—*you* are the expert. Reporters need someone like you to explain the details of a story. They are always looking for a fresh angle and for experts to help them create a great story under intense deadline pressures. As I've explained in Chapter 3, the quality of reporters' stories determines their reputation and space allocation. Remember this: *The media need you!* It cannot happen without you. By providing data or research, you offer reporters credibility and accuracy.

You can become the media's trusted source—the expert. The media need your knowledge of your industry. You follow and understand trends in order to serve your clients or customers. The media will never, in a lifetime of reporting on your industry or profession, be able to match the level of knowledge you acquire by handling simple problems related to your work every day. Clients' frequently asked questions create patterns that can be turned into dynamic story ideas for the media.

THE INTERVIEW

If you know your subject and are confident, you can handle the most difficult questions any media contact may ask you. In fact, you may find the experience enjoyable and satisfying, perhaps even exhilarating. And because of your background and knowledge, you have an unquestionable advantage over your interviewer. You're on your home turf, and you know the topic better than the interviewer.

Don't be afraid to get excited about a subject. Watch good speakers: they have head movement, eyebrow movement, and hand gestures. If you just sit stiffly and give monosyllabic answers in a monotone, the producer will be reluctant to use you. Know such technical rules as not putting your hands in front of your face or showing examples outside the frame of your shoulders—you'll surprise the camera operator and lose the shot. Regardless of the subject matter, the media are trying to create an exciting show. Use descriptive, not technical, language so you don't bore the audience.

Summary of Interview Tips

- Be confident. You have more knowledge of your subject than the journalist does.
- Be straightforward, pleasant, and cooperative. Look and sound professional.
- Know what you want to get across in the interview. Know your facts. Know the good news and positive aspects of your business.
- No question should come as a surprise. In fact, you'll probably be able to think of more questions than an interviewer can.
- If a question you're asked is unreasonable, the listening or reading audience recognizes that and won't expect you to dignify such questions with a response.
- Never speak off the record.
- Never say anything negative about another member of your industry or firm.
- Don't keep talking to fill dead air on a radio or television broadcast. You have no obligation to keep the interview moving. That's the responsibility of the journalist or interviewer.
- You're under no obligation to reveal information that is damaging to you or that is helpful to a competitor.
- Have one or two memorable comments written down. These will cast you and your company in a good light.
- Make positive points to your advantage regardless of the pattern of the questioning.
- If a television or radio interviewer interrupts without allowing you to answer fully, the audience will sympathize with you.

- Just by virtue of being interviewed, you develop instant credibility and importance. Knowing that the media need you will give you confidence when speaking to them.
- Don't try to develop a different persona during media interviews in an attempt to become what you think you should be. Rely on the strong points of your own character, personality, and experience for the raw material.
- Stress the positive aspects of your company, your cause, or your ideas. Emphasize good news and helpful information as much as possible.
- Think problem/solution. Think of the problems in the industry and the solutions that can resolve them.
- Long, rambling answers and comments should be avoided. Keep your message simple. Comments should be brief and to the point so they can be easily understood by the general public. If you do this, your words are more likely to be remembered or written down, and you'll have more time to make your points.
- Don't use jargon. If you must use industry-specific terms, take time to simplify them or provide definitions.
- It's always better to say something important more than once than it is to say several unimportant things.
- Don't try to make too many complex points, especially in a television interview.
- You are not in the interview to defend yourself, so don't allow yourself to get into that position. Worse yet, don't assume it.
- Don't be afraid to not answer a question, but explain why you can't. Viewers, listeners, and readers don't expect anyone to know everything. Not knowing everything shows your human side and adds credibility. You can say something like, "I don't feel qualified to answer that" or "I don't have the complete data at this time."
- Don't be sidetracked. Hold your ground. Don't allow the interviewer to take up valuable time on matters unrelated to your goals.
- Never lose your temper or shout or yell. Always remain calm, but stay firm in your comments and always in control of yourself.
- Don't volunteer information or opinions that may damage you.
- Refute incorrect statements immediately. Correct any statement that is inaccurate, especially if the statement weakens your position. This can include statements made by other guests, audience members, or callers. If you do make a meaningful error, admit it. Apologize quickly and then go on.

- Don't let the interviewer misinterpret your statements. Politely interrupt and set the interviewer straight about your meaning.
- Once you've fully answered a question or made a point, stop talking. Don't be pushed into adding unnecessary words.
- Don't be suckered into hypothetical or leading questions. Just turn to the interviewer and say, "I wouldn't want to speculate on that."
- Provide evidence that supports your points and plans. Be prepared with charts or props that you can use.
- Develop anecdotes, quotations, or metaphors that can make your stories come alive. People love stories. Think of that killer anecdote story about what happened to one of your clients and how the solution solved a problem for him and can do the same for media readers, listeners, or viewers.
- Have a ready supply of illustrations, charts, and, in the case of TV, film clips or videotape for television producers. You want to call ahead of time and find out if they can be used.
- For direct television interviews, you shouldn't have notes on paper. You want to relax and not read prepared answers or statements.
- Have fun with the interview.
- Don't allow distractions, such as crew conversations and background noise, to throw you.
- Show genuine emotion. Get excited. Laugh; show surprise or indignation if something arises that you don't agree with. But don't let emotions cause a flood of words. That can distract your message or image.
- Don't be afraid during an interview to repeat a key point, maybe in a slightly different way.
- Always try to simplify your comments and answers; and try to have the last word in a television or radio interview.
- Don't allow the interview to end on a negative note that is detrimental to you or your interests.
- Sit still and in place at the end of a television interview until you get the off-the-air sign. Don't make any additional comments.

After the interview, the first thing you should do is thank the people involved—the interviewer, the production manager, and so on. Most of the time you'll be motivated to do this; you'll probably be exhilarated. If it's a print interview, ask the writer if you may read the interview before it's published. Politely make it clear that you're only checking for accuracy in what you said or what you didn't say that you might like to add. Usually, writers won't give you the chance to read the article, but it's worth asking. It's also a good time to contact your client list and let them know that you've been interviewed—by whom, for what medium, and when it's going to run or air.

After the interview, especially a relatively short one, you may feel let down. The tendency then is to second-guess yourself, but don't waste time doing that. Get busy with after-interview activities. Contact other media—print, television, or radio—for additional exposure. If you now have an audio- or videotape, you can send it to other stations.

Contact the journalist who interviewed you and ask if your photo is needed. Have professional photos taken and always on hand in your media kit to send. Keep a journal of each media appearance, writing down the pertinent information—what worked and what didn't, what charts you took with you, and whether you used the interview for reprints. Also, keep track of the people who interviewed you. Sometimes they move in and out of other media outlets.

MEDIA RELATIONS POLICY FOR YOUR FIRM

You don't have to be a large business to have a media policy. A little planning ahead can avert crises and save time and clients. A media relations policy spells out ahead of time who in the firm may respond to media inquiries, what kinds of information can or should be released to reporters, and what information must be kept confidential.

Establish an accurate public perception of who you are and what you do. As I've noted previously, reporters need you as a source of news and background information as much as you need them to give you publicity and clarify your point of view.

A good media policy should include most or all of the following elements:

- List (by name or position) who in the company may respond to media inquiries and, for those who are not so authorized, to whom firm members should direct media inquiries.
- When you talk to a reporter, remember that you're really talking to the public.
- Treat reporters, editors, and program directors courteously. Their impression of each individual in your firm, all the way down to the receptionist, affects their impression of the entire firm, and that may influence how they report about you.

- Return reporters' calls within an hour, if possible. They are usually on tight deadlines, and they appreciate (and occasionally reward, i.e., call on you again) promptness.
- Explain to the media who you are and what you do, just as you would at the end of a written news release. Prepare a brief statement to which all authorized firm members can refer. Aside from that brief statement, don't try to promote yourself. Just answer the questions.
- Speak in plain English that average readers and listeners can understand. Avoid jargon, legalese, or bureaucratic language.
- Describe in your media relations policy what kinds of data or information must remain confidential.
- Feel free to ask the reporter questions about the story (e.g., What's the theme? What's the point of view? Who else is being interviewed?).
- If the reporter asks for information that is already a matter of public record, don't hesitate to share it (unless there is some compelling reason not to). Withholding such information will only force the reporter to develop other sources; and you want to be a valuable source.
- Always be truthful and accurate. Never exaggerate or inflate. Understatement usually works better than hyperbole, especially when dealing with experienced (i.e., cynical, skeptical) journalists.
- Do not speculate. If you don't have personal knowledge about a subject, help the reporter reach a source that does, even if that source is not a member of your firm.
- If you need time to research or think about how to answer a question, it's all right to tell the reporter that you need time. Ask what his deadline is, and then assure him that you'll call back with an answer before that time.
- Never disparage other firms.
- If you cannot answer a question, make sure the reporter understands why. Don't simply say, "No comment." It could be interpreted as evasiveness. Instead say, "I'm sorry, but this matter is the subject of a pending lawsuit" or "I'm sorry but I'm legally obligated to protect my client's confidentiality."
- Keep it simple.
- Unless you're an experienced public relations professional, assume that everything you say to a reporter is on the record. If you don't want to see it in print or on the air, don't say it.
- Don't argue with the reporter.

- Don't ask the reporter if you can review the story before it's published. If the story is highly controversial, you may ask the reporter during the interview to read back your quotations to confirm accuracy.

A clearly written media policy can help to minimize your firm's media liabilities and promote a positive public perception of your business—it's all in what you say and how you say it.

15

How to Get on Radio and TV

Odds are that you still remember CNN news coverage of Operation Desert Storm and General Norman Schwarzkopf pointing to one of his oversized charts during his nightly briefing. It wasn't an accident that his four-part color charts were easy to read and available to the press. Today's military knows how to make a memorable presentation in the media. It places so much importance on it that officers must receive a passing grade in media presentation to be graduated from the Army's General Staffs College. The ability to make a successful presentation has also become a prerequisite for advancement in business.

Our society rewards those who are willing to risk becoming highly visible by creating a *celebrity* effect. Those who understand this already utilize the media to maximize the rewards. The good news is that media visibility can be achieved by businesspeople. (See Figure 15.1.)

It's easier to be seen than you think! There are 74 million viewers watching any one of the big cable networks at any given time. There are five new cable stations going up around the world every week, and the industry is very competitive. "Television stations and news organizations are hungry for content, but producers can't spend the countless hours required to become an expert on a subject—they'd rather just pick up the phone and make a call to someone who's already an expert," says Bud Brutsman, a producer of documentaries for the History Channel.

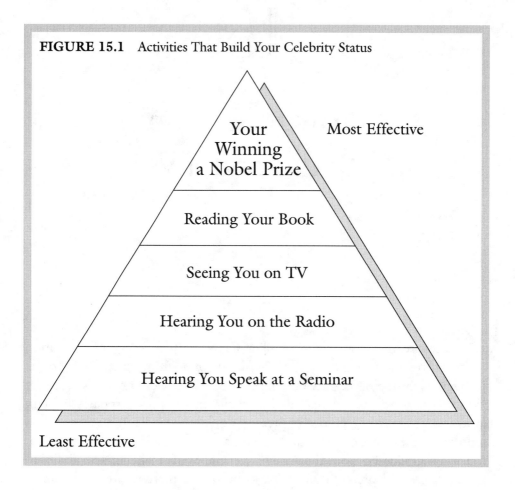

FIGURE 15.1   Activities That Build Your Celebrity Status

Your Winning a Nobel Prize — Most Effective

Reading Your Book

Seeing You on TV

Hearing You on the Radio

Hearing You Speak at a Seminar

Least Effective

MEDIA PERSUASION

Don't approach them with information borrowed from another magazine or repackaged common industry knowledge. Although most people make the print news in their hometown with an announcement of a new vice presidency or a new office opening, this kind of news won't get you on the radio or TV. Brand new information is what the media are looking for. It has to be exciting enough that a programmer looking through jaundiced eyes says, "Wow, I didn't know that."

A brief interview has a longer-lasting effect than a carefully worded announcement.

Radio and television shows differ in the topics they cover and therefore the type of guests they look for. Nonetheless, there are some basic steps you can follow that will increase your chances of getting on the air. First, review the profiles of many shows carefully to ensure that your pitch is appropriate for a particular show's format and style. Talk shows often gather ideas from major newspapers or industry trade magazines.

Watch the shows that you're most interested in appearing on. That will give you insight into the host's style and interests and also help you determine if you should pitch to them. Don't suggest appearing to talk about your product or service. Producers don't care what you do—they *do* care about creating exciting or informative segments and shows. So try to sell the producer on why you'll be a great guest—you're someone who'll provide something of value or interest to the audience. Don't worry; the producer knows you're selling something and will usually make sure you get a plug. But you have to get on the show first!

Many of the same tactics used to get into print also work for other media. Adapt your query letter and proposal accordingly:

- Query if there's interest in what you're offering.
- Write a proposal.
- Write out a script.
- Become a reliable source.

If you write articles and/or books, speak at associations—in other words, become an icon—the media will find you.

MEDIA SOURCES

How do you locate the more than 10,889 radio stations in the United States? Or have them find you?

Following are a few directories to help you reach people who can create business-building news coverage:

Publicity Blitz Media Directory-on-Disk   800-784-4359
Bradley Communications Corp., publishers of *Radio and TV Interview Report* and other publicity resources.

Bacon's Media Directories   800-621-0561
Include most media outlets in the country. Available in libraries and on CD-ROM.

Burrelle's Media Directories   800-631-1160
Individual directories for print, radio, television, and cable.

Buy a listing in *The Yearbook of Experts, Authorities and Spokespersons,* says yearbook editor Mitchell Davis (*Broadcast Interviews Source,* 2233 Wisconsin Avenue NW, Suite 301, Washington, DC 20007, 202-333-4904 or <yearbook. com>). For a cost of $605, you are listed in the directory; more than 8,000 copies of this publication are distributed annually to newspaper editors and program directors of national and local radio and television. Information is indexed by topic and geographic location.

Also, North American Precis Syndicate (NAPS, New York, 212-867-9000) has a feature release service, Radio Roundup, that goes out to 3,000 radio station writers and television news and talk shows. The cost is $2,650, with an estimated average 200 to 300 placements.

DEVELOP A RADIO/TV MEDIA PRESS KIT

Don't waste money on fancy media kits; less is more. Make them simple and to the point. You can buy double-pocket portfolios at any business supply store that provide space to include a cover letter, media release/fact sheet, a biography, any previously published articles, and a photograph, as shown in Figure 15.2. These are the primary materials producers use to evaluate potential guests when making booking decisions:

A – Cover Letter. Your opening paragraph must immediately grab their attention and tell them why you (or your product) would be a compelling guest or segment. Posing questions and answering them, and quoting statistics are two ways to make strong, convincing statements.

B – One-Page or Two-Page Press Release or Fact Sheet. Highlight aspects that provide more in-depth information about your hook. This single sheet may also announce an event or something significant that involves your

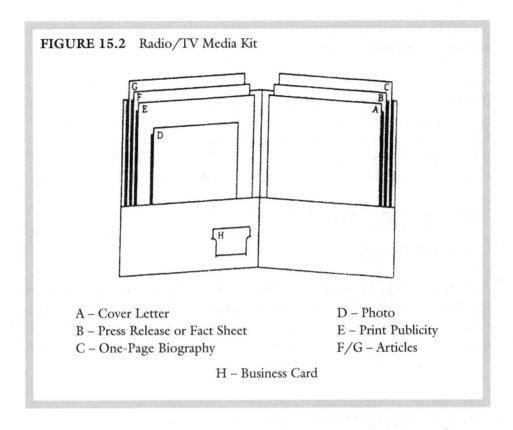

FIGURE 15.2 Radio/TV Media Kit

A – Cover Letter   D – Photo
B – Press Release or Fact Sheet   E – Print Publicity
C – One-Page Biography   F/G – Articles

H – Business Card

product or service. Follow with an overview of your service or event and its special significance to the public.

C – One-Page Biography. This should list your professional credentials as an expert. Don't send a résumé. A bio can be more conversational and lend validity to your expertise in a certain area or subject. Be sure to include previous media appearances.

D – A Professional Photograph. Your publicity photo should be an eight-by-ten-inch glossy black-and-white headshot—or a shot of yourself at a seminar event with lots of clients milling about or in another work-related situation. Newspapers can use your publicity photo along with their story on your business. Any photos in your media kit should be by a professional photographer. Only when a photograph is professional looking, in focus, and presents you in a good light is it worth a thousand words! Don't ruin all of your efforts by using an ordinary snapshot.

E – Print Publicity. If you have clips from magazine or newspaper articles that were written about you or your product, include a few of the most favorable, but avoid sending clippings from country club newsletters or church bulletins. Also include recent high-profile articles that are relevant to your topic. Publications such as *Newsweek* and the *Wall Street Journal* can help get a producer's attention and add significantly to the credibility of your pitch.

F/G – Articles or Anything You Feel May Help.

H – Business Card.

Additions that could make a difference. Compile a list of at least ten questions that the host or interviewer could ask you during the show or segment. Pitch a general topic or segment idea, but show how your information and expertise can be applied to create other kinds of segments. For instance, the author of a business book can do separate segments on:

- How to make smart decisions in the real estate market
- Should couples buy homes in this volatile economy?

Don't overstuff your media kit. Overstuffing will make your kit look sloppy and unprofessional. Use a padded mailing bag or small box to mail your media kit and product sample so they arrive in good condition. *Don't* send videotapes of previous media appearances.

Get feedback. Sometimes your message can be contrary to the image you wish to convey. Ask someone to look at your kit and give you an honest opinion. Is it too much of a sales piece? Better to hear it from a friend than to not hear from an editor.

Additional tips for your media kit. Be certain that your packet presents you in a way that will enhance your image and open opportunities. When you provide editors and producers with an attractive media kit, you impress them with both the quality of your work and your presentation skills. If you present detailed information in print and communicate with flair, you assure them that you will be able to communicate with their audiences in a highly satisfactory manner.

The more you reveal in your packet about your credibility, the appropriateness of your presentation, and the appeal of your public persona, the more you assure producers and editors that presenting you and your story will be pleasing to their audiences. You need to convince them that you will help them with that agenda. In addition, reporters are always in a hurry and appreciate thorough digests of information about special products or services that preclude their need to research facts or devise focus points. You can assist this process by including a list of highlights that might interest the audience. You do editors and yourself a favor by making it easier for them to present your topic.

This is your opportunity to go beyond a simple press release and create a concise and attractive package of information that represents and supports your point of view. It can, therefore, greatly improve your chances for placement in a publication—or even get you onto a local TV show.

TELEVISION'S MOST POPULAR BUSINESS SHOWS AND CONTACT NAMES

TIP: Talk shows like CNBC's *Business Tonight* often use investment professionals or panels consisting of several guests on a given topic. Producers spend a lot of time and energy creating panels. Offer a ready-made show to a producer by suggesting other possible panelists.

Oprah Winfrey Show

Harpo Productions
110 North Carpenter
Chicago, IL 60607-2146
Phone: 312-633-0808 or 312-591-9595
Fax: 312-633-1515 (n/v)

Airs: Monday–Friday, 60 minutes (For time, consult local listings.)
Audience: Primarily adult women

Profile: Syndicated women's program with controversial social issues, interviews, and guests

How to Pitch: Oprah is doing less sensational topics and more shows about positive relationships, family, and home topics. Proposals have to go through research and then be deemed interesting enough to be pitched to a producer.

Booking Contact: *Senior Producer* Ellen Rakieten

BookNotes (C-Span)

400 North Capitol Street, NW #650
Washington, DC 20001-1511
Phone: 202-737-3220
Fax: 202-737-3323 or 202-737-6226

Airs: Sunday, 8–9:00 PM CST
Audience: General adult

Profile: Interview show featuring nonfiction authors and commentaries on books dealing with public affairs and history

How to Pitch: Only hardcover, nonfiction books are used. Authors must be able to sustain a full hour of conversation. Send all info by mail.

Booking Contact: *Senior Producer* Hope Lamdy (202-626-4601)

CNBC Network Programs

2200 Fletcher Avenue
Fort Lee, NJ 07024
Phone: 201-585-2622
Fax: 201-585-6393

Business Tonight

Airs: Monday–Friday 6:30 PM–7:00 PM EST
Profile: Business news program for executives who want to keep on top of important issues

How to Pitch: They look at pitches for segments involving corporations doing things differently. Faxes are the worst way to communicate. Mail is the best, preferably very short, one-page pitches.

Booking Contact: *Producer* Robert Ferrarro (201-585-6366)

Money Wheel

Airs: Monday–Friday, 10:00 AM–4:00 PM
Audience: General adult

Profile: Business, finance, and consumerism show with interviews and guests. Takes listener phone-ins dealing with personal finance. It is produced by most of the same people who produce Market Wrap on CNBC.

How to Pitch: Material should be sent through the mail, and the pitch should show why the guest's information can benefit the audience.

Talent: *Correspondent* Sue Herera (201-585-6465)

Market Wrap

Airs: Monday–Friday, 4:00–5:00 PM

Profile: A review of the day's financial market activities

Booking Contact: *Producer* Dan Clark 201-585-6343

Moneywise

Produces regular personal and family finance segments for *CBS News* and *CBS This Morning*. This show wants everything from personal financing and budgeting to investment information and opportunities.

Senior Producer: James Segelstein (212-975-8907)

CNN

P.O. Box 105366
Atlanta, GA 30348-55366
Phone: 404-827-1500
Fax: 404-827-1593

Audience: General adult worldwide

Profile: CNN broadcasts various news programs all day between its other programming.

How to Pitch: Programs include general interest books and authors. If you are pitching a book or topic in the area of food and health or business, contact the appropriate producer/booker.

Assistant Director of Booking: Diane Durham 404-827-1320. She's the best contact for books and authors.

News Assignment Editor: Peter Ornstein

CNN Programs: Before Hours/Business Day

5 Penn Plaza
New York, NY 10001-1878
Phone: 212-714-7848
Fax: 212-714-7962

Airs: *Business Day*—Monday–Friday, 6:00–7:00 AM
Audience: General adult business people and investors

Profile: Business news programs with up-to-the-minute reports on issues, money management, and people. Also guest interviews with primary interest in interviewing prominent investment fund managers and analysts.

How to Pitch: Producer Dan Bases prefers that you fax your information to him first and then follow up with a phone call. Keep it short.

Booking Contact: *Business Day Producer* Alex Kaufman (212-714-7848), 9:00–11:00 AM

Today

NBC-TV
30 Rockefeller Plaza
New York, NY 10112-0002
Phone: 212-664-4602/4249
Fax: Won't give out

Airs: Monday–Friday, 7–9:00 AM
Audience: General adult

Profile: News and topics of general interest; morning magazine show with interviews

How to Pitch: It's best to pitch through the mail unless the subject or guest is breaking news.

Booking Contact: *Book/Literary Editor* Andrea Smith (212-664-4371)

CBS This Morning

CBS News
524 West 57th Street, Suite 44
New York, NY 10019
Phone: 212-975-2824
Fax: 212-975-2115

Airs: Monday–Friday, 7:00–9:00 AM EST
Audience: General adult; over 3 million per show

Profile: An information-based broadcast covering breaking news, weather, business and personal finance, consumer affairs

How to Pitch: Mail or fax your material to the producer who handles your subject. Producers want "nonflashy" press kits and materials that are complete and give them plenty of time to present.

Booking Contact: *Book and Supervising Producer* Carol Story (212-975-4112). She's the main contact for books, authors, and features. She's open to most ideas. Be sure to send complete press kit and comprehensive background information on the guest/author you're pitching.

ABC World News Tonight (ABC-TV)

ABC Inc.
47 West 66th Street
Second Floor
New York, NY 10023-6201
Phone: 212-456-4040
Fax: 212-456-2795

Airs: Monday–Friday, 6:30 PM EST
Audience: General adult

Profile: Hard news show with coverage of the day's world events; authors used in this segment

National News Desk Editor: Ms. Kris Sebastian

NBC Nightly News

30 Rockefeller Plaza, Room 324
New York, NY 10122-0035
Phone: 212-664-4691
Fax: 212-664-6044 (n/v)

Airs: Monday–Friday, 6:30–7:00 PM EST
Audience: General adult

Booking Contact: *Researcher* Tammy Fine. Send her information on experts and authors.

16

Add Entertainment

Entertainment is something added to the mix, but it's not the mix.

The traditional media model has historically had a church-state firewall between content and advertisers. The press is supposed to be objective. Newspapers and magazines are credible because they're independent; companies buy advertising space—they don't tell the press what to say.

Today, companies are creating mediums of expression to make their own marketing and advertising more effective. Most businesses face a stark choice: incorporate elements of existing media into their companies and products or go out of business. The sales pitch is the script and the CEO is the star. First it was Michael Bloomberg, and now Charles Schwab is the latest media mogul. In-house media gurus suddenly have as much to do with a company's viability as advertising gurus once did. Today's company wants to get above the clutter and avalanche of media products. Customers want to receive the highest-quality experience and the best information. The media business has shifted to accommodate.

In a recent article titled "Why Charles Schwab Is the Newest Media Mogul" by Randall Lane in *Worth* magazine (March 2001), Lane reports that Schwab's broadband shows suddenly have the potential to reach 63 million viewers—a viewership that dwarfs CNN's financial programs and Bloomberg Television combined. Schwab's printed articles have the potential to overwhelm the *Wall Street Journal, Forbes,* and *Worth.* If you visit Excite, MSN, or

SeniorNet Web site, you'll find Schwab content and tools. Check out *On Investing* magazine, a one-million-circulation quarterly produced and associated with Bloomberg that's sent to Schwab's richest clients. Being visible is a way to provide value-added products and services.

The corporate culture is driven by change, and the market is, of necessity, driven by competition. That's why advisors and consumer businesses have to develop their own media model. For example, in the past the brokerage industry aimed at keeping information out of the hands of individuals. Power was in the information that was kept under lock and key. That's changed. Competitors are scrambling to copy what Schwab has successfully demonstrated.

Today, Schwab has 7.4 million customers and collectively holds $1 trillion in assets with $10 billion of new business each month, according to Prudential Securities analyst Eva Radtke. That's why Schwab paid so much for its AOL partnership. Today, Schwab's physical plant resembles the organizational structure of a typical media company. Schwab relies on an emotional connection as its strategy for using media models to convert and retain customers.

When Schwab began its Internet presence, it flooded channels with targeted banner ads, but business generation from ads was lousy. Advertisers need to tell a story, which can't be done with banner ads. When Schwab began placing content with the banner space, the ads generated a response rate of more than 1 percent. An article on managing retirement funds along with a banner touting IRA services running on Senior Net doubled the response rate to 2 percent. The highest response rate recorded by Schwab was 24 percent for an article that ran on the American Association of Individual Investors site. Now Schwab is convinced of the value of the concept of using actual stories, chats, streaming video, and message boards—not as saleable products but as visceral marketing tools.

Much of Schwab's success comes from casting itself as a neutral source for information and emphasizing that the best place for your account stems from the enormous credibility of Charles Schwab himself. Polite and personal, his low-key approach to television commercials has created credibility among investors and translates well into creating trustworthy communication. Visitors to Schwab's site are welcomed in a way that feels like a Disneyland audio animatronics' welcome or Microsoft's annoying animated "helpers" that come to your rescue.

The bottom line of the Schwab concept is to use content to cement and protect relationships with its best customers. Schwab created a signature service for the top 20 percent of its users—those with more than $100,000 in assets—by using the media to impart privileges. Like Frequent Flyer gold membership, most of the media perks are invisible to the general Schwab audience. They're not aware of the quarterly magazine with content from both Schwab and Bloomberg, nor do they hear about the video broadcasts, such as the CEO-speaking series and such regular features as Intel's Andy Grove.

That the Schwab strategy is relationship driven and "value added" is apparent as Schwab himself talks to a small group of investors who have access to an exclusive area of the Web site. This access is delivered courtesy of Schwab himself, who issues the invitation personally; it's a kind of access not even big name media sites can deliver.

Lower on its pyramid, Schwab skews its content heavily toward how-to, analysis, and expert advice but stays away from breaking news. On the practical side, this avoids the need to create an army of reporters, as Bloomberg or Reuters have done. On the emotional side, this slant allows Schwab to cast itself in the role of advisor, which, of course, makes the reader more likely to become a client.

The idea that a better-informed account holder is more likely to be an active investor has led Schwab to accumulate an archive of 2,000-plus articles. How-to articles, which are very popular on television and in magazines, are particularly effective on the Web, where suggestions can lead to immediate transactions.

Schwab has also launched a learning center on its Web site where visitors can access up to 10 educational courses (20 will be available soon). Each is tailored to adult learning patterns and takes about an hour to complete, covering everything from selecting mutual funds to determining risk profiles. The courses are self-directed and allow the user to apply the knowledge immediately via tests and mock trading. The user is generally invited to try the real thing. It saves a lot of time and money because it's not face-to-face. During the recent market turndown in 2000, more than 200,000 people entered the Web shop and registered for online classes. When the markets got rocky, the pace of those registrations spiked over 40 percent.

Schwab's content-based outreach also targets specific niches. Learn from I-Village, areas for women, tracking interest in tax issues, and Turbo Tax, which, of course, lead back to Schwab's site. Schwab also offers an 800 number where advisors are available to answer questions.

Stocks and bonds cannot be touted on Schwab's Web site; compliance officers monitor every word and picture. But at the end of the day, Schwab doesn't really care if the customers are coming back solely for the reading or watching or listening to its media products—it wants them to come back to trade.

17

The Web Play

I'm no expert about Web sites; I haven't felt the need for one yet. I've taken a wait-and-see approach, watching big companies spend millions of dollars designing and perfecting their Web sites, only to see no return on their investment. The Web is a wonderful place for communication and gathering information, but there's also a lot of misinformation and trend setting.

All I can say about it is that if you do have a Web site, you can write problem/solution articles on the site. But having a state-of-the-art Web site isn't necessarily going to build your credibility. It's easy to test what works and what doesn't on the Internet. Simply answer the obvious question: How many customers have you gotten from your Internet site?

You may have noticed a lot of advertising on television a few years ago trying to push people to the Internet to purchase goods and services. What is your own experience with that shopping place? How many products and services have you bought on the Internet? How many times has the experience *not* been satisfying, the information outdated or not refreshed for long periods, or delays common?

Just two short years ago, everyone was racing to add dot-com to their name. Some did it to secure funding; others were fearful of being left behind or thought of as dinosaurs. For whatever reason, the environment has changed. The media are gloating over the Internet failures—the love affair is apparently over.

As the second era of technology consolidation begins, the Internet still remains an important strategic channel, but companies are less focused on Web-only products and more on the Web as part of their bigger picture.

Aside from communication and research, you're back in the same boat when it comes to sales and marketing that every advertiser faces: How do you get *your* message seen, heard, and read? There was a time when simply converting a company brochure into a Web page was enough to get you noticed, but that doesn't cut it today. The key is to differentiate yourself from the 900,000 new pages that appear on the World Wide Web each day. Use the AltaVista search engine to identify Web sites that contain the words you call yourself, and then count the matches. The noise on the Internet is increasing all the time.

Marketing on the Internet used to mean building a brand sexy enough to excite and entice, and communications were about short-term success; today, it's long-term survival. This current dot-com downturn may be a breakthrough for the right credibility marketers. When you look at your Web site, consider what problems your customers have and how your product or service solves them? Is that apparent on your site? If not, rework your site.

If you're simply displaying a Web page and users happen to come across it, the chances are they won't be ready at that moment to make a buying decision based on your service or product; and you won't have made enough of an impression to motivate them to come back to you when they are ready. If you want to know exactly who is looking at what pages on your site, Amicus Networks (512-418-8828) has a product called "Community Builders," which reveals the user's name and e-mail address, so making contact becomes easy. Anonymous users are not part of the network; qualified users are. That's a great head start.

One important way to differentiate yourself is to focus on developing a sense of community, because commerce has always occurred within a community. In the heyday of the gold rush, for instance, commerce was born when enough miners were in one place to support a tavern. A post office would be established when there was a critical mass to support that, and so on.

You can interact, and bond, with a community on the Internet, where users are interested in the services and products you offer. That means answering people's questions, interacting with them, and delivering your marketing message calmly, without shouting and without worry from competitors. The challenge is to develop an online community that includes both your clients and prospects, and that's in alignment with your marketing plan and goals.

An Internet consultant found that customers still rank interactive communication the number-one criterion for an online system. This would include news reports, chat rooms, and e-mail plus audio and video broadcasts. If you like what you see when you surf the Web, you look a little further; if you don't, you hop to another place. Interactive communication alters that by allowing a two-way communication flow where people can get questions answered and real needs addressed. That's what survey respondents reported they're primarily looking for. Don't design a site without facilitating some form of interactive communication.

HOW TO GET STARTED

- *Step One*. Allocate time over the next couple of months to just browse. Spend time exploring various Web sites. Look for what you would like to display on your own site.
- *Step Two*. What is the "unique selling proposition" that will not only differentiate you from your competitors but will position you as the market leader in that niche?
- *Step Three*. Build your Web site. You will not get it right the first time. The Internet is constantly changing, and your site should as well. Plan a systematic review every few months to see how effective it has been and what you can do to improve it.

The publishing industry was worried about negative effects of the Internet on publishing, but the Internet has had the opposite effect. It has actually created greater demand, and there are more magazines and books than ever today. Web sites are just online magazines with no real subscribers, no delivery, no way to get people to come back. Today, with 2 million commercial Web sites to choose from, you can be virtually certain that people will not find yours. One other little problem: 50 percent of all searches result in a failure. Vast numbers of people are using a search engine, but any single Web site is a very tiny needle in a very huge haystack.

STAGE FOUR

■ ■ ■ ■

EXPANSION

18

Getting Published

Someone approached me at a seminar where I was about to talk about credibility marketing and said, "The last speaker told us how to write a virtual article. You just write an article and then copy it with the masthead of a magazine as if it were published. With today's new publishing software, you can make it look *real*."

When I addressed the group, I pointed out that "looking real" wasn't credible—it's fraud. And if you're going to bother to write an article, why not try to get it published—*really!* Fear of rejection stops most people.

TASK ONE: STUDY THE PUBLISHING BUSINESS

To demystify the publishing process, I recommend that authors attack the process the way they would any other part of their business life and approach it in a very businesslike fashion. If someone started an athletic shoe company, for example, he'd first find out who the competitors were, who the manufacturers and retailers were, and so on. He would examine the business.

Examining the business is a step that very few writers actually take—they're trying to produce something for an industry that they have learned nothing about. The more they study the publishing industry, learn what works, what doesn't work, how it all happens, who plays what role, what kinds of things are working in other businesses, the better. The publishing business is a competitive one. Once the *Chicken Soup for the Soul* books caught on, other publishers started putting out collections of positive, feel good, inspirational stories. That's what happened with the *Complete Idiot's Guides.* The people at MacMillan capitalized on the *for Dummies* line in the same way. If the public is interested in a topic or style, chances are other publishers are going to want something similar.

Certainly, people need to have a good idea for a book. To find out if your idea is a good one, move out of your circle of comfort. Don't just ask friends and family because they'll tell you it's great. Ask somebody in a bookstore. If you've got an idea for a business book, introduce yourself to the people who are in charge of doing the buying for that section at the local bookstores. Ask for their professional opinion of your idea. They have no reason not to give an honest opinion. And they may tell you that there are already four other books like that or that your idea was hot a few years back, but it's now outdated. You can glean a lot of information from people who work in bookstores and get honest feedback and opinions.

In *The Complete Idiot's Guide to Getting Published,* Jennifer Basye Sander explains the six habits of highly successful writers. When she asks audiences to name the number-one quality needed to get published and they shout out "Talent!" and "Inspiration!," she has to stop them and tell them, "No, it's *persistence.* It doesn't have anything to do with talent or creativity. It's the ability to decide that this is what I'm going to do, and just keep working until you make it work."

Read the writers' trade journal, *Publisher's Weekly,* for about $170 a year (800-278-2991) to help you get a finger on the pulse of the industry, to see what's working and what's not. A couple of times each year, a roundup article of business books appears, and that one article contains complete information about what has sold well in the last year as well as what's coming out. It's competitive research. The different segments of the industry are examined at length: health, travel, cookbooks, and so on. If you are loathe to pay the subscription fee, chances are the local library has a subscription.

It's also helpful to talk to people in bookstores to find out what kinds of books sell and who asks for what. Also pay close attention to the bargain tables in bookstores because those are books that haven't worked, and you don't want to be proposing an idea similar to what's sitting on a bargain table. Such rejects are overpublished areas and outdated ideas—the flops that you need to familiarize yourself with so you can avoid them.

As in any other business, it's a good idea to attend industry conferences whenever feasible. People go to writers' conferences for the purpose of meeting editors and agents so that a few weeks later, they can send a note to an editor saying, "I met you at the South Carolina Writers' Conference, and you encouraged me to send my proposal." It's that face-to-face contact that can separate you from the hoards of letters that arrive.

TIME LINE

Once you've decided what to write about, then put together a proposal and go shopping for a publisher. There are two ways to do this: either go directly to publishers yourself or find an agent to help you. If you're going to do this yourself, take the time to research and find out which publishers buy the kind of book you want to write so that you don't waste your time or theirs. Once you identify publishers that you'd like to submit to, try to reach their acquisition editors to read your proposal. Their job is product development.

What happens after you submit your proposal? Usually between 30 to 60 days is a realistic amount of time to expect some sort of response. You'll either get the "no thank you" letter or the publisher (or editor) will call and say, "I'm interested in taking this project to the next step." The next step is presentation to the publishing committee, for which the publisher will use your proposal as a tool to sell the project to his team. The results of that meeting will be a decision whether the publisher will extend an offer. If you get that far, you will then negotiate a contract.

Negotiating the Contract

A publisher's offer usually consists of an advance against royalties. Contrary to popular belief, an advance is not intended to replace your normal income or to make you rich. It does two things: (1) it indicates the publisher's level of commitment to a project, and (2) it offsets some of the costs involved with writing a book—the advance against royalties. Royalties are the money paid on each copy of the book sold. A royalty is usually a percentage of the publisher's list price or a percentage of the retail price. Some publishers pay on what they collect and others pay on the list price of the book. Royalties are a long-term proposition, with the intent that the book will continue to sell consistently or sales will increase over time, allowing the author to continue to make money.

Everyone has a different perspective. From an agent's perspective, the higher the advance, the stronger the commitment from the publisher. After the advance is paid, there are no guarantees on sales, so it makes sense to get as much money up front as possible. What authors don't realize is that publishers sometimes have to cut into the marketing budget or publicity budget to come up with a larger advance. No pool of money is available that publishers can offer as an advance—it's a project-by-project thing—and the project pays for the advance. Paying one author a higher advance has nothing to do with how much the publisher will pay another author. But a successful book has a lot to do with how it is marketed, and the more money the publisher can spend up front to market it, the better.

Lower your expectations and examine the reasons that you are writing the book. The advance just covers the cost; it's not the goal. Maybe the publisher that pays the lowest advance is going to be the one who promotes your book the most aggressively.

HOW YOUR BOOK IS PUBLISHED:
BEHIND-THE-SCENES WORK

Inexperienced authors usually think that their acquisitions editor is the only person who works on their manuscript, but that is seldom the case. In fact, that person likely does the least amount of editing. Your acquisitions editor may suggest changes, such as putting Chapter 4 before Chapter 3, but the real editing is usually done by someone else, a copy editor, who possibly is outside the company.

The writer works with the acquisitions editor to develop the manuscript and when that process is finished, the manuscript goes to the managing editor or to a production editor. When you submit the final manuscript, you should feel that you'd be happy if it were published the next day just as it is. Although it's going to get a lot of cleanup in production, you should be comfortable that you don't need to make any substantial additions or changes.

The managing editor handles the production of the book from the time the manuscript is finished until it goes to the printer. It is the managing editor's job to determine what level of copy edit the manuscript needs and to assign it to the copy editor for conformance to the publisher's style and for a thorough check of grammar, punctuation, and spelling.

At the same time, the managing editor also looks at the manuscript in terms of how much time must be spent styling the manuscript and setting up the preliminaries for the design. The manuscript is then sent to the art director, who will either give it to an in-house staffer or send it out to a freelancer to design the book. In either case, the art director needs to know exactly what the elements in the book are—if special pieces of art are included with the manuscript and, if so, whether they can be used. There is often a designated page length for the manuscript based on the publication packet and "pro-formas" that the editor carries out before the book contract is signed.

As soon as the book comes back from the copy editor, in usually about three weeks, it is sent to the author for review. The author is allowed a week in which to review the edits. The copy editor provides a section of notes to the author mentioning any inconsistencies. For instance: "Dear author, this was a little bit unclear—did you mean 'time' or did you actually mean 'thyme'?" The author will have a chance to respond to such notes, so you can expect to see and be able to address technical or mechanical issues after the copy edit.

During the author's review, the design is being finalized. Once the author's changes are entered and the design finished, everything is compiled into one copy of the manuscript, including any artwork, and is sent to the typesetter. There's usually a first-pass galley that you'll be given a chance to take a look at. The typesetter has about four weeks to produce the page proofs. Then the managing editor makes copies and sends them to the proofreader (to read against the manuscript), to the indexer, and to the author (to review). Page proofs are already broken into pages exactly the way they're going to appear in the book as opposed to galleys, which are continuous pages of type without page breaks. Running heads, page numbers, and so forth are already formatted in the page proofs.

The author generally has another week to review the page proofs. The indexer may be given a couple of weeks because indexing can be done at the tail end of a project. When the author and proofreader submit their changes to the managing editor, the changes are compiled into one copy and returned to the typesetter for the final corrections. After another week or so, the manuscript will be returned to the managing editor, who does a final quality check to make sure that all corrections have been made.

Finally, the book goes to the printer. Depending on whether it's bound in soft covers or hard covers, the printer will have the book for four to six weeks.

During that time, the printer will send bluelines (or digital proofs) to the managing editor before printing. The term *blueline* refers to a process in which film is made based on the pages and submitted files, and the film is exposed onto light-sensitive paper. It comes out blue, and the pages are put together to look exactly the way they are going to look in the published book. It is still possible at this stage to make final corrections, but it is expensive to do so.

Sometimes a situation arises where a manuscript is very late, and the schedule must be compressed to meet commitments. In that case, the author may have to forfeit one or two editing reviews. You can expect the entire production process to last six to nine months.

Ideally, enough books are printed in the first run to cover a year's time, but if a book "takes off"—creates an unexpected demand—it's sent right back to press for a second printing. The sales director stays in close contact with the sales reps and knows how books are selling. If a book is selling well, reprints can usually be out in three weeks. The make-ready work has already been done, and the printer simply needs to schedule time to get it on the press.

At the end of four to six weeks, copies of the book are shipped to the publisher's warehouse until they're released to bookstores. Usually, the copies aren't in the warehouse long before being released—maybe one or two weeks. Bookstores usually have the copies on the shelves sometime in the following month—it could be one to three weeks after receipt depending on their work volume and how hot the title is. At this point in the process, you need to take off your writer hat and put on your promoter hat to make yourself available for interviews. Initially, you were working alone on your own behalf; now you have a partner—your publicity efforts are supplemented by the publisher.

The publicity campaign starts ramping up simultaneously with the production process about three months before the book's release. Timing is critical because, of course, the books have to get on bookstore shelves, but they also have to start moving off shelves immediately in order for the bookstores to continue restocking. The day a new title hits the stores, people must be out there looking for it; otherwise, it will be pulled to make room for others. The publicity campaign can't start too soon because people will be looking for a title, but they'll forget about it if they can't find it. On the other hand, the publicity can't start too late because the copies will have already been pulled by the time people are looking for them.

SELF-PUBLISHING

Getting published is a business project just like any other business. Although I don't normally recommend self-publishing, it has its place. If you can't get a publishing company interested in you, and you decide that it is in your best interest to have a book, go ahead and publish it yourself. If this is important in getting to the next stage of your career, then it's a part of your career you need to invest in just like anything else. If the book is to be used primarily as a handout, a tutorial, or a product that you intend to sell directly, then the only thing stopping you is the cost.

Self-publishing has limitations, such as the lack of professional critiques through editing, but the biggest limitation is the lack of distribution. Ninety-nine percent of people who self-publish can't get the same kind of distribution a publishing house, with a professional in-house sales team, can. Publishers also have sales rep groups selling a book to accounts in their region. On top of that, they have a rights manager who's negotiating licenses for translation rights, paperback rights, reprint rights, and audio and video rights.

It's possible to get into a retail chain of bookstores, but be prepared to front the costs of shipping and selling your book. Unlike other retail businesses, books are 100 percent returnable. If a clothing shop has trouble selling a certain item, it marks down the price until it's gone. But booksellers who can't sell your book put the copies in a box and return them to the publisher for full credit. And if you are selling a softcover title, they tear the front cover off before sending them back for credit. According to industry figures, the average bookstore sends back approximately 20 percent of its books.

COSTS OF PUBLISHING A BOOK

The costs are different for every book project. There are manufacturing costs: paper, print, and binding; and production costs: copy editing, proofreading, project management, page layout, and design work. These can be anywhere from $50,000 up into the $250,000 range depending on the numbers of copies. The publicity budget is different for every book based on a book's potential. There's a co-op expense for any cooperative effort with bookstores. That's always an unknown until the time the book is being sold and the bookstores decide whether they're interested in that sort of marketing campaign. There are overhead expenses: time, computers, phone bills, and faxes to everyone on the book's publishing team and sales reps working on the project. See Figure 18.1, which shows the basic costs of book publishing.

FIGURE 18.1   Costs of Publishing a Book

The Seven Basic Costs of Book Publishing
(Based on an average-length $25 hardcover)

Manufacturing: 10% ($2.50)

Distribution: 8% ($2.00)

Marketing: 7.5% ($1.87)

Overhead: 8% ($2.00)

Author Royalties: 10–15% ($2.50–$3.75)

Retailer Discounts: 40–50% ($10–$12.50)

Profit (Before Returns): 1.5–16.5% ($.38–$4.13)

How-To Sell Your Book

Sales Projections

Projecting sales is an inexact science. And it's different for each product. Sometimes a book is so similar in substance and form to something published in the past that projections can be based on a comparison; but times and trends are a factor. Other times, a book is so leading edge and so new that the publisher looks more closely at the statistics about the market. Sometimes, the publisher is unfamiliar with the topic and seeks the advice of customers and people at key accounts.

Initial sales projections were low for a book called *Rags to Riches: How Ordinary People Achieved Extraordinary Wealth* because it was perceived as soft and wasn't a how-to book—as most Dearborn books are. One of the factors that contributed to the success of the book was that the authors were self-promoters. The book also got some attention from Oprah Winfrey, which helped sales. Mary Good, acquisitions editor for Dearborn, states, "There are things that you can never anticipate—and others that you just hope for. Our sales projections and our financials are always based on the expectation that we're going to do everything we possibly can do and we're going to do it all right. But given that that's our standard for all of our efforts, some things just are better, easier, and faster than others."

Publicity

It's important for authors to do their own publicity in whatever ways they can. Because no one is going to care about a book as much as the author does, an author may do well to hire a publicist. Publicists receive bound copies of the page proofs when they're available at first pass, and they send them out to reviewers three to four months before the book's publication date. Magazines often work three to four months ahead of schedule. Television shows and NPR (National Public Radio) also need a long lead time. NPR and Oprah are two of the biggest publicity factors that influence book sales. It's possible to hire an outside publicist for just one area of publicity such as radio or TV. The publicist needs to be sure that a book fits the demographic of the audience for a particular show and pitch books that are appropriate for a specific program.

Evaluate what a publishing house can offer and decide if it is the type of publicity you want and whether it is enough. A small publishing house might be able to offer authors more personal attention than the larger houses. The larger houses may not have the staff to offer personal attention to authors, although they may hire an outside publicist for their major authors or books. They will put together a complete campaign, launch the book, and, once the book is out, they will pass it on to an outside publicist to keep things moving.

The type and amount of publicity provided by a publishing house often depend on the type of book—the subject matter and how wide a reach the book is expected to have. Some books are promoted strictly through a print campaign, pitching all print applicable to the topic, because the books don't lend themselves to sound bites or television or radio.

A book can become extremely successful if the publicity is targeted to the appropriate market. For example, when Dearborn published a book called *Secrets of a Millionaire Real Estate Investor*, the publicity efforts were aimed primarily at real estate columnists and radio programs focusing on the real estate investment community. Sales were helped by the author's efforts and some great reviews by some very influential syndicated real estate columnists. The author is well connected in the real estate investment community and helped the publicity effort tremendously through speaking engagements. He did a lot of talks to real estate investment groups, which are always hungry for new information and new techniques. He also spent a couple of hours on the phone calling colleagues, friends, and others he knew in the real estate community telling them about his book. Then he did an NPR real estate program in Ohio. All of a sudden, the book landed on the *Wall Street Journal*'s best-seller list.

Radio is a very powerful medium because it's inexpensive and interviews can be done from the author's home. It isn't necessary to travel, but if the author is on a promotional tour, interviews can be done from any location or in any time zone. And if the author keeps the publicist apprised of his or her travel schedule, the publicist can work to set up local media promotion. Many bookstores and libraries welcome local or visiting authors for book signings and talks.

With business books, it's easier to pitch a story to business journals that have a local connection. Borders has corporate sales reps in various stores and these reps try to encourage local businesses to buy copies of books. One Borders is doing a networking night called "Corporate Night," where four local businesspeople are brought in to do a short talk. Discount coupons of 20 percent are given to the audience.

The challenge of publicity is to figure out the hook or interesting story and how to get the media interested. So many people publish books that the mere fact that you're an author isn't newsworthy. Anything an author can do on a local level is helpful and frees the publicist to do the things that need to be done on a larger scale.

19

A Winning Book
Query Letter

You don't have to have a completed manuscript to sell your book!

Selling implies that you have an already created product. Most writers (and nonwriters too) spend hours at the keyboard trying to produce a sellable manuscript; then they wonder who wants it. It's like writing a letter and then asking, "Whom should I send this to?" What you really want to do is find out what the publisher and editor want—and then write about that. Spend your time writing a good query letter first. Otherwise, selling your writing can be extremely frustrating.

Write inquiries to publishers to find out if they'd be interested in your book concept before you start the writing process. Not only does this technique save you time and energy, but when you get a publishing contract, it really motivates you to finish your book. In the sample query letter, you'll see that I'm not selling the book—I'm introducing myself and inquiring if they'd be interested in even reading a proposal.

First, look up your target market. *Writer's Digest* has a listing of various publishers and basic information on their magazines' needs. Entries are packed with formatted information and points to look for that will maximize chances for querying successfully. Some of the things to look for are limited circulation, a specialized audience for distribution, large percentages of freelance material, and/or a stated desire to work with new writers.

Occasionally, guidelines will outline information about the type of book to write. Here is a sample book query letter:

Keep your query letter brief; one page is the ideal length. Editors are extremely busy, and they're more likely to read a one-page query letter. Essentially, you must convince the editor that it would be worth his time to publish your book. Why is your information new and different? It's important to get

---

Dear Editor, (use his/her name)

On April 1, 1946, an earthquake struck the Aleutian Islands of Alaska. It was deep in the ocean floor, and the quake's enormous shock immediately began to travel outward. And even though the two-foot swell spread throughout the cold Pacific, many fishermen didn't even notice the swell beneath their boats because it was traveling so deep in the ocean, moving at a jet speed of 550 miles per hour. In less than five hours, the wave struck the Hawaiian Islands, thousands of miles away. For a moment, the wave caused the Hawaiian coastal waters to rush out, leaving boats and fish stranded on bare sand. Then the waters reformulated to a massive tsunami that came crashing into the island's shore, destroying everything in its path.

I'd like to propose a book idea that would cover the repercussions of earthquakes. The book will be approximately 280 pages and can be completed in six months. If you're interested, I'd like to send you a formal proposal complete with a table of contents, an outline, and sample chapters.

Please contact me at (   ) or by e-mail at:

Warm regards,

Larry Chambers

your idea across quickly and succinctly. You want to interest the editor in your topic, not overwhelm him. Whittle your idea down to the bone so you can summarize it in one or two sentences.

In subsequent sentences, you can explain how you developed the premise, how many chapters it will take to cover the topic, and the chapter headings. In addition, editors like it if you can provide photos, artwork or sidebars, and graphs or charts. After less than 30 seconds of reading, the editor should have enough information to make a decision: the subject, the focus, the essential details, the content, and the length.

No need to worry if you've never written before. Just tell the editor your qualifications.

Agent Sam Fleishman gets an average of 100 submissions a week and looks at possibly 5. His advice: "The query has to serve an important purpose; it has to get me excited about that book. An individual may have a terrific book, but they [sic] have to establish the excitement immediately. If they can't do it in a query letter, which is relatively simple, I have to wonder whether they can do it in a book."

Make a list of a dozen or so publishers who might be interested in your book. Try to learn as much about the books they publish and their editors as you can. Research and a professional approach are often the difference between acceptance and rejection. You will likely receive some rejections, but don't give up. Rejections in the book publishing business are like hang ups to a cold caller. Send your query to the next publisher on your list. Multiple queries can speed up the process. Personalize your query by addressing it to an editor. Never send a form letter.

WHERE DO YOU FIND EDITORS AND PUBLISHERS?

Writer's Market is a directory of over 8,000 editors' names and addresses and what they publish.

The Literary Marketplace is a fairly expensive book ($200+) published by R.R. Balcher. It lists names and addresses of publishers, literary agents, book packagers, and printers—everybody who's involved in the book publishing industry. A prospective or aspiring writer shouldn't necessarily buy one, but it's in almost every library in America.

You'll find listings of hundreds, if not thousands, of publishers and what they publish. You *can* go directly to publishers, but it's much more efficient to approach a smaller number of literary agents who know the cast of characters and what those editors are looking for.

The Literary Marketplace includes probably 30 or 40 pages of literary agents and their address, phone and fax numbers, and e-mail address as well as what area they specialize in. Send a query letter to half a dozen agents saying, "This is my idea, and this is why I'm qualified to write it. Are you interested in helping me sell it to a publisher?" You may get more than one taker, but select just one as you don't want two people selling the same thing.

Try Smaller Publishers

Literary agent and president of James Peters Agency Bert Holtje suggests a look at smaller publishers. The big trade publishers are the ones who are demanding celebrity names, but smaller publishers are willing to take a chance on an individual. However, most of the smaller publishers don't often work with agents, simply because they can't offer much money up front. It becomes a double bind and puts an agent in a tough position. If an agent sends your book to a smaller publisher, it sends up a red flag: "Here comes an agent with a book—he's going to want a lot of money—so don't even look at it." But if the book comes in over the transom, smaller to medium-sized publishers almost always look at every submission they get, whereas the larger publishers immediately send proposals back saying, "We deal only with agents."

Cooperative Publishers

Cooperative publishers are not self-publishers, but I've included some in this book. Cooperative publishers look at your book in terms of its merits, and you help in the publishing cost of the book.

Other Options

I personally don't think self-publishing is the best way to go, as I noted earlier. I don't think you should buy someone else's book and slap your name on it either. I see ads in the back of industry magazines urging people to "Become an Author Overnight"; this means someone pays $12,000 or so for his or her name to be put on a book cover as the author. This is deceptive—the opposite of credibility marketing. Why not get help from a ghostwriter if you can't write the book yourself? If you can't explain your process, you ought to learn how. When I ghostwrite, my clients still have to input their own ideas and thoughts. I help arrange their words into an interesting book, but the words are their own.

Go the Distance!

The best thing an author can do is work with the publisher to promote his or her book. Speak on the topic, write articles or editorials, and coordinate that with the publisher's publicity department. We recently published a book called *Loyalty.com* with an author who was going to be speaking all over the world. We coordinated his tour schedule with our international offices in 39 countries around the world to create a global promotional campaign and made sure we had inventory in each of the key markets. As a result, the book has shown up on the Amazon.com best-seller list fairly consistently.

SUMMARY

Here are some insights that can help you get your book published:

- *You* can go directly to publishers.
- You don't have to have a completed manuscript to sell it.
- Know your material and facts well.
- Publishers are not after get-rich-quick books; they are looking for an interesting angle or a new twist.
- Smaller publishers are willing to take a chance with authors with good ideas even without prior writing credentials.
- Do your research in your local bookstore. Look for books on topics similar to yours; find the book editor's name in the acknowledgment section of the book and make a note of it. Now you know the name of an editor who may be interested in publishing *your* book. Success *does* leave clues.

■ ■ ■ ■ ■

20

How to Write a
Book Proposal

Think of the book proposal as a sales brochure. Publishers buy 90 percent of their nonfiction books based on proposals. If you can write a good proposal and it sells the book before you write it, you should have the incentive to finish. The more work and time invested in the proposal, the easier the writing and publishing process will move along.

There are three key topics focused on in a proposal: the author, the book, and the opportunity. No one is as strong an expert on the topic and as knowledgeable of the market for a specific book than the author. Because the proposal is a sales tool that the editor uses to sell the project to the sales team, marketing team, publicity people, and publisher, the more support you provide for the existence of the market, the relevance of the topic, and the need for this book in the marketplace, the better.

The sales director is going to be looking for different things. When a sales director goes to Borders and pitches a book on credibility marketing, he needs to be able to tell the buyer how *Credibility Marketing* is unique or different from other books. *Unique* or *different* can mean a new slant, some way of looking at a topic that no one has thought about before. What often differentiates a book is that it's packaged for a new audience—an online investing book, for example, may be targeted to beginning investors or to women investors or to socially conscious investors. And if your tentative title doesn't obviously identify your targeted readership, it's important to convey that information in your proposal. Include a comparison of key competitors.

And to take that one step further: Any sort of media hits or print placement adds credibility to the author, but even something on the topic by a different author helps. If an author has a portfolio of published articles or a media kit documenting lots of exposure that matches two or three hits that are in line with whom the publisher would target with the book, even better. It could mean the publisher's market reads that magazine or watches that television program or listens to that radio program, and that further strengthens the editor's sense that this author is in front of our readership.

But keep things fresh. I think any publisher considering a book proposal wants to make sure it's not information that has appeared elsewhere—that it's not recycled information. Everything's based on research and secondary sources, yet the way it's presented and packaged should be different and have a new slant. A survey of books in print will determine if anybody else has already approached your subject and, if they have, help you add your own spin and your own ideas to old ones.

BOOK PROPOSAL GUIDELINES

Say you just got a positive response to your query letter. The next stage is to build a 20-page to 60-page proposal. Its purpose is to sell your idea and your credibility and platform, as well as emphasize the need in the marketplace for your material. The book proposal will also force you to assess whether your book is marketable without wasting a lot of time.

Use the following guidelines when preparing your proposal. It will ensure that you provide all the information needed to review your proposal fairly and quickly.

The book proposal should include:

- A cover letter
- A table of contents
- A detailed outline or a sample chapter of at least ten pages
- An overview of the project
- An author's biography

The Cover Letter

The cover letter should include:

- A brief description of the book, in 20 words or less, that tells the who, what, and why
- A list of top competing titles or top sellers in the same genre
- A statement of how you plan to help promote the book—endorsements, conference exhibits, as a lecture tool

Write a brief description of your book in two or three sentences, in which you explain the concept of the book and its intended market (reader). What prompted you to write the book now? It's important for you to be aware that this brief description will later turn into a sales hook that the publisher's sales force will use to pitch the book to bookstore buyers and people in other key accounts. Hook editors with the first few words by skillfully planting attention-grabbing highlights with a few mouth-watering phrases: "Every millionaire spent years making the same six critical mistakes. This book will show the reader how to avoid them. In our recent tech stock boom, the percentage of millionaires in the United States increased . . ."

The Table of Contents

The table of contents enables the editor to see your entire focus at the outset. Be sure to include appendixes, glossaries, and the like. If the book will include any special features (e.g., blank forms, case studies, photos or references to recent research, and the like), provide a separate index. Develop a list of descriptive chapter titles, but make them intriguing or fun—not too textbookish. Be creative—not hokey. This is where you could use clichés that are usually scorned in creative writing. At bookstores, examine several books' table of contents to see what attracts your attention; then mimic that style.

The Outline

The outline should expand the table of contents to include subheadings within each chapter and also a brief description of what the chapter is about, such as what the reader is going to learn in each chapter. Don't be too brief to adequately represent the project.

A sample chapter is helpful but not absolutely necessary. If you've already started writing, include something that is representative of your work on the topic. This will serve to help reduce any concerns the editor might have about your ability to deliver quality work beyond the proposal stage. If you don't have a chapter written, just send a sample of any other work that you have. If you've been following the steps in this book, you have already written an article, which can be used for this purpose.

The Overview

The overview should be a longer description of the book from one to three pages and more like the text in a jacket cover that expands what you said in the cover letter: its purpose, approach, organization, and promotion. Include the following:

Who **the book is for and why you targeted that audience.** Describe the primary and secondary markets for your book. Where appropriate, indicate both the general type of reader (e.g., people interested in real estate) and the specific type of job or function held by the reader (e.g., bank mortgage lender). You wouldn't state, "My book is for wealthy individuals." You need to be more demographically sophisticated than that. It's great when authors can provide statistics to support their information. Any statistics, anecdotes, examples, or anything else that can help quantify and further illustrate the existence of the market is very helpful.

One statement publishers completely discount is "Everybody in the country's going to read this book." But if an author says, "My primary audience is investment advisors, and there are 600,000 investment advisors in the country," a publisher may think, If I could just get 1 percent of them to read this book, it would be a best-seller. But statistics are less important in helping make sales projections and more important in just establishing the market. For example, the publisher will realize that if there are 600,000 financial professionals, they must have publications and associations, and that's where they will focus their publicity.

What **the book is about and what makes the book different from, and better than, every other book on the subject.** Be as specific as possible about what information you plan to provide. This is a good place to include why you are the expert and what motivated you to write the book. If you're not sure, now's a great time to ask yourself why you're doing it.

One publisher likes to hear that the author is writing the book out of a desire to share knowledge and expertise. And publishers also want to hear that the book project fits into the author's business plan and marketing plan, and that it is an extension of a larger effort to spread the word about a topic. A lot of authors are afraid to say, "I'm writing this book to help market myself," because it might sound like a wrong reason, but, in fact, it's exactly the right reason.

Why **the book is important, useful, and necessary.** Justify the book's commercial appeal. Describe what aspect of your book's content will sell it. What problem does it solve? What question does it answer? How will it benefit the reader?

Who **the competition is.** Include titles, authors, publishers, and dates of publication. Amazon.com is a great resource for finding competitors and similar topics. It's a mistake to think or pretend that there is no competition in your area. Although it may seem as if having no competition would be a good thing, the publisher doesn't see it that way. The publisher wants to know there are other books out there on your topic, because that indicates there's a market for the book. If there is nothing out there, the publisher's first question is, Why not? It could mean that this is a first market opportunity, but according to Dearborn acquisitions editor Mary Good, that only happens in rare cases:

> A book that I acquired recently on peer-to-peer technology had no direct competitors at the time. There was nothing on that topic, but that only lasted for two months. Even in that case, it's not fair to say there's no competition—there's indirect competition, other books out there that the reader browsing the bookshelves might buy if your book weren't there.

How **you plan to help promote the book, including media contacts, applicable associations, conference/lecture schedule, and the like.** This should indicate your level of commitment and your confidence that there is a need/market for what you have to say. It is critical to identify all existing sales and marketing opportunities. Things are changing so fast in the publishing industry and information is available in so many different formats and places that soon many publishers will no longer rely on bookstores as their primary outlet.

Publishers have to be creative and look for every possible opportunity to leverage their contacts. If your book contains a mention of a specific trade publication or magazine, you might interest that publication in doing a review of your book. You should point these things out to the publicist or salesperson. Be sure to mention any potential readers who might want to use the book as a calling card and might be planning to buy multiple copies. Do you have a client list to whom the book could be sold? Include a marketing example of numbers and whether you could obtain a commitment from a special group to purchase a specified number of copies. It may also figure into the total financial picture of the project.

The Bio—All about Yourself

Information about the author is almost as important as what the book is about. The author's bio is where you inform the publisher what experience or professional credentials make you uniquely prepared to write this book. Have you published other books/articles/columns? Include your educational and professional background and achievements, any association/organization affiliations, and any media attention you've received. Write it in the third person.

THE OVERLOOKED

Always keep a copy of what you are sending!

Appearance counts. The proposal should be double-spaced, of letter quality on bond paper. Make sure your proposal isn't dog-eared, marked up, or otherwise abused by a previous reader. No editor wants to get something somebody else has read—it means it was rejected.

How long will the manuscript be? When will it be completed? If you are writing on a computer, provide details of any formats and/or special software you're using.

Attach a headshot of yourself. Also, if you have any news articles supporting the popular interest and relevance of your topic, attach them to the book proposal. When your publisher sees that a magazine editor bought a story on this topic, it adds credibility.

Contrary to common practice in other industries, editors do not prefer bound proposals. If an editor likes your proposal, she will want to photocopy it; binding it is only an impediment. It is best to use a paper clip to secure the pages.

Start obtaining the appropriate permissions as soon as you make the decision to include material from another source; sometimes it takes months to get a reply. You wouldn't want production of your book to come to a standstill if you found you couldn't use something already typeset. Immediately begin assembling a permissions folder containing all related correspondence that you will submit with your completed manuscript.

21

Design Your Book

WHY A BOOK?

Everyone has a reason. For me, there is nothing like the pride I feel walking into a bookstore and seeing one of my books on a shelf.

You know it moves you way up the visibility ladder, builds your power image, and helps you leapfrog over your competitors. But have you considered that your book's real mission is to explain how you work with customers/clients? Your book becomes a special calling card, which accomplishes three objectives. First, it eliminates the question of who you are; second, it explains your process; and third, it makes it almost impossible for anyone to forget you.

Here is the hidden bonus! The process of writing a book will help you clarify and develop your own business theory. It helps you see and deepen your own understanding of what you do. You discover what you are passionate about. You'll find it satisfying, and that will give you the motivation and energy needed to excel at what you're doing. Your enthusiasm will influence you, and you, in turn, will influence your prospects and clients.

Can you imagine seeing your business card in every bookstore in the country or on the Internet? Imagine handing a prospective client your book. One you wrote. It gives credibility to *your* thoughts and ideas. The distinction of having written a book separates you from the rest of the pack; it's the antithesis of the way most of your competitors operate. If used properly, a book can become your ultimate marketing tool, providing a recurring stream of new prospects and clients.

Take the book you're reading right now. The cover not only has my name displayed on it, but inside is included a way to contact me. I have to buy copies to hand out, but think how I can use them. Offer a free copy of your book as a marketing tool during seminars. For very little extra cost, you can have extra covers of your book printed. These overruns can make high-quality, high-impact, inexpensive brochures—with strong copy and good design on the reverse side of the cover; they make powerful mail-out pieces. Include testimonials from clients who are big hitters in their field.

A book is almost impossible for anyone to throw away. My clients keep my book on their bookshelves or credenzas, or close at hand, where they can refer to it easily. And most important, the publisher paid me to write it! To become an important book, your story has to have valuable consequences for your community, city, nation, or the world. If it does, it will transcend the private arena and your story will become public and universal. Don't editorialize, preach, psychologize, or explain more than necessary to prove your theses. Just explain your industry problems, offer practical solutions, tell what and how you do it in your industry, and how it helps your customers. Following are some basic elements for writing a book.

OUTLINE

Some writers feel outlining limits their spontaneity and leads to dull writing, but making an outline enables you to write your books as fast as possible. Good writers always start with an outline. The outline is the structure. Realize that structure creates the surface design that's going to carry the book. If the reader doesn't recognize any structure, that's okay—the structure isn't supposed to be visible to anyone not searching for it. Readers should simply feel a natural, almost inevitable, movement toward fulfillment, as if they've achieved a true understanding of the subject.

We can no longer remember what we've read as a part of a chain of events. We have only a vague impression but no sense of expectation or why the last chapter relates to the third chapter. But if a book is laid out correctly, a curious thing happens after you finish reading it. You only remember the accumulated effect, so the order of narrating is critical. After we finish reading, all events exist together in a single moment. In other words, chapters have to be in the right order or we would feel no reason to go on to the next chapter.

Continuity from one chapter to the next is needed. Readers must feel that the chapters are connected—and they're connected by transitions. One feeling of satisfaction in reading any book is trying to figure out just how in the world the writer is going to bring all these far-flung ideas, theories, and elements together in some way to make perfect sense—when all of a sudden, about three-quarters of the way through the book, you feel, Aha, I finally understand how that works.

MATCH YOUR REFERENCE MATERIAL TO YOUR OUTLINE

Label a folder for each topic and fill it with the articles, reprints, and permissions you have collected. Organize your research material before you start writing, so that you know what you are including and where to find it. Highlight each section of your outline with different colored markers, and then go back through your reference material and highlight important information and quotations to match your outline. You may find some information is applicable to more than one section or is more effectively used in a different section.

Name Its Parts

Step 1: Give your book a title that tells what it is about. This is more to keep you focused while you're writing, as it may be changed later by the publisher.

Step 2: Break the title into four or five chunks of information. These could be sections or parts similar to this book. For example:

Part One: How to Build a Credibility-Marketing Program
Part Two: How to Research Your Market
Part Three: How to Get Media Play
Part Four: How to Get Your Book Published
Part Five: How to Keep It All Moving Forward

If you turned these how-to titles around, they become the five major questions you have to answer when building your visibility.

Step 3: Break down each part into four to six smaller, manageable pieces or chapters. Create major topics; then break down each topic into subtopics. If it's a how-to book, break each subtopic into steps that the reader can perform.

The average book is going to be about 280 typeset pages. You will need more than 360 double-spaced manuscript pages with extra pages for charts, illustrations, a glossary, and such. By dividing the book into five parts with six

FIGURE 21.1   The Design of a Book

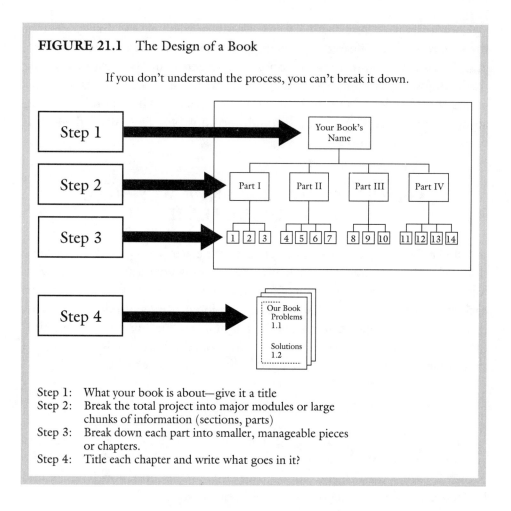

If you don't understand the process, you can't break it down.

Step 1:   What your book is about—give it a title
Step 2:   Break the total project into major modules or large
          chunks of information (sections, parts)
Step 3:   Break down each part into smaller, manageable pieces
          or chapters.
Step 4:   Title each chapter and write what goes in it?

chapters, each chapter has to be only about 12 pages. The chapters don't have to be the same length; some will be lighter than others. I always set page goals—not time goals. If I say I'm going to work on this book for eight hours, it means nothing if at the end of eight hours, I have only one page. I learned this trick a long time ago from Leonardo Bercovico, the head of the UCLA writers-in-progress courses.

Step 4: Title each chapter and describe what goes in it—that is, outline the key points. Each chapter should contain one sentence describing a central theme or present a problem. Your job, then, is to solve the problems, thereby answering the premise of the book.

Once you see the outline, you have much more freedom to relax and allow your book to surprise you.

STRUCTURE

Structure is the most important element of the writing process—the foundation that keeps you on track. In the writing process, structure holds everything together toward a major focus. Simply put, structure is the relationship between the parts and the whole. This can be illustrated by the assembly of a sound system. Certain component parts—an amplifier, pre-amp, tuner, speakers, cassette deck, and so on—are connected to form a working system. How good or bad the system is (the whole) depends on the quality of the components (the parts).

Just as with a speech, you introduce a book, develop it, and conclude it. That's the foundation for all successful writing. Within that broad structure are other elements, such as the logical development or linking of ideas, transition, pacing, and so on.

You can include anecdotes or case histories, as I frequently do, to illustrate your point. It helps the readers relate to the problem in a personal way and keeps them reading to find the solution. You may want to sprinkle what I call *confidence builders,* or encouragements, such as, "You can easily follow this advice," throughout your book to keep readers from feeling overwhelmed.

As you start to define, or set up, your article or chapter, decide what your slant will be or the point that you want to get across. The more complicated the subject, the more time you may need to give readers the information they need to become interested. The first ten lines of your chapter establish the direction, tone, voice, and pace. From the first line, hit your readers over the head and get their attention.

You could close with another colorful anecdote, this time with a positive outcome that portrays an opportunity. It may include a call to action, which is an alternate approach to telling your readers that they are now ready to act on what they have learned. I sometimes include a "quick start" list, something like "Five things you can do to start your investment program."

RESEARCH

Rule number one is to know what you're writing about. The best books are firmly grounded in research. Research brings knowledge on the facts and focuses the writer outside of himself beyond a personal perspective. Don't be a cocky expert. You don't always know what you're looking for. When you begin, start researching your subject, and in the course of your research you may discover a much more fascinating line of inquiry.

Break through the paralyzing inertia we all experience at the beginning of a huge project. The first thing to do is go to the library or Internet to look up some facts, which will help you get started. Be prepared to muddle around, browse, and get lost but then find your bearings. It will save valuable time in the final draft. It's okay to feel confused, disappointed, even dismayed, but stay doggedly focused and determined to hunt down whatever you need wherever it exists, and you'll probably discover more than you dreamed possible about your subject.

Good research can add knowledge, power, and authenticity to your book, helping the reader understand and more fully participate in the industry that you work in. Research can take you beyond the cliché, beyond generalizations and oversimplifications and the usual sales and marketing pitfalls. It takes you beyond easy assumptions that are normally just spit out and not proven. If the book is comprehensive, research will be even more important. A detailed chronology can be the background for the manuscript.

Design a research plan. This can be as simple as scrawling a list on a piece of paper or setting up a calendar—brief or detailed. It can remind you of what you'll eventually need to learn to accomplish the project: the plans, the starting point, a working paper to be refined and revised as you go to keep you on track. Because the nature of research is discovery, the plan will evolve. Sometimes you'll cross-reference, track down ideas, and make some unexpected discoveries, accidental finds, and surprising facts that ambush you. This will let the reader come away with what everybody in marketing is saying they'd like to do, which is create the *Wow* effect.

Begin telling people what you're doing; collect ideas. Immerse yourself in archives, interviews, documents, existing research material, subjects that might prove valuable; refer again to notes, essays, published articles or stories, or that first draft that's been sitting in the drawer. Cast the net far and wide.

Organize the research; create a filing system that makes sense to you. Sort the notes, documents, charts, and transcripts into appropriate folders. Don't just make notes; make notes about the notes, and have a place to store the overall information. The job of research is connecting the dots and assembling seemingly unrelated facts into a pattern, a matrix of meaning that becomes the backbone of your book.

STYLE

Technical Writing

In a how-to book, most of what you'll be writing is technical writing: how radar works, how to sail a square-rigged ship, how to climb in an expedition, how a swordfish boat sets its gear. Unless your readers are also experts in the profession or experts on the subject, it's all a technical subject to readers. That goes for sports, cooking, politics, medicine, psychology, accounting, consulting, anything. So take the time and thought to teach readers what they need to know about the subject. Technical writing gets inside the mechanism of the subject at hand. If you're not an expert on a subject, so much the better. Go to people who *are* experts and listen to what they have to say. Read their reports, their biographies, and their memoirs; ask them for diagrams and pictures; and ask dumb questions. Repeat their answers in your own words.

Integrate the knowledge so you don't bury the reader. In *Writing a Book That Makes a Difference,* author Philip Gerard says, "The two principles writers should follow are to present factual information in bite-sized pieces, not massive doses, and to integrate statistics and descriptions, science, history, and so on into the context of the story—not just free-floating information but information that heightens the chapter, the overall book." The information can't be dry or abstract; each new fact must heighten readers' appreciation for the next moment in the narrative.

Folksy Narratives

Bill Nelson, a financial advisor from Cayton, Ohio, is one of the all-time great storytellers. He also produces well over $2 million a year. When he talks to a customer, he doesn't go into a lengthy lesson on taxation. He'll say something like this:

Let's say you want to cross a lake as quickly as possible. You have a choice of a 300-horsepower jet boat or a pontoon boat with a 20 hp motor. The thing is, the 300-horsepower jet boat has a three-foot hole in its hull. Which boat would you choose? The supposition is that it doesn't matter how big the motor is, you still have no chance of making it to the other side of the lake because you've got a hole in the boat. And taxation is the hole in your asset accumulation boat. Unless you patch the hole, you're never going to reach your goal.

This folksy way of talking also makes for great writing. What Bill does so well is to enter into the world of everyday people and take them from their context back into his world of solving tax problems. He never got technical or wordy, but you get the point.

POLISH

Writing is rewriting. The more time you spend polishing the manuscript, the better the book is going to look in the readers' hands. My favorite saying is, "Writing that doesn't keep you up all night won't keep your readers up either."

Inexperienced writers tend to include absolutely everything they have learned—every fact, every impression, and every quotation. That's okay, but there's a test for these facts and anecdotes that you learn from your research. Can readers relate to the way the information is presented? Is it essential to understanding your subject? Does it move rather than impede the story? Does it amplify the important theme without causing confusion? Is it unique rather than redundant? Nonfiction is similar in structure to the framework of a novel, but instead of scenes within each chapter, there are questions that get answered and concepts that get defined. Each one should have a clear reason for inclusion.

After you've written a first draft, read it out loud, paying attention to the nature of your story. This is a time to rearrange and to correct mistakes, redundancies, omissions, clumsy transitions, and trivial things. When you read it out loud, see if it sounds both true and profound. Does the intention of what you're trying to write come across? Have an assistant or friend read it out loud (or you can record it), so you can hear what's missing, such as writing in passive voice, which slows the continuity.

Cutting isn't as hard as you might think; more difficult is trying to fill in what's missing. Make sure all the parts fit together and reinforce the intention. Readers need to clearly understand all the facts; otherwise, they can't enjoy the context of the book. The important thing to accomplish in a first draft is completeness, a sense that it's all there, so there are no holes in the subject you're covering.

Passive Voice

I can't help it, but I make this mistake all the time. It's almost impossible to write without using the passive voice, but trying to is a goal worth striving for always. Look for opportunities during your rewrite to make your writing more active. Passive sentences are nearly always longer than active ones and they can dull your writing. Passive writing makes for passive reading. To engage your reader, transform passive sentences into active ones.

John F. Kennedy was shot by Lee Harvey Oswald on November 22, 1963. That's about as bad as a sentence can be. On November 22, 1963, Lee Harvey Oswald shot John F. Kennedy. That's considerably better. Another example is, "A law was passed." That makes it sound inevitable. Instead, write "Congress passed a law."

You produce the active voice when you use the standard subject-verb-object, "John hit the ball." We create a passive voice when we invert the rule to object-verb-subject, making it, "The ball was hit by John."

PATIENCE

For many writers, the process of putting it all together comes naturally and instinctively. Others, however, become overwhelmed and seek the help of ghostwriters—people who give you all the credit but write the book themselves. Keep in mind that ghostwriters typically charge a lot of money; they're seldom experienced in your industry and don't speak your "language." And, perhaps most important, they don't share your passion for the topic.

Don't be in a huge hurry: if you don't know what you're going to write, wait and it will come to you.

22

The Master Book Template

Over the years, I've noticed similarities in how-to books. I read every new one that hits the stands. Not just how-to books but self-help, psychology, home improvement, and the art of fly-fishing—the gamut. All seem to follow a pattern that publishers know will sell. So why not follow a proven style?

The following master book plot presents ideas on how a nonwriter can achieve a professionally written book that inspires readers to want to put ideas into action.

STEP 1—THE PROLOGUE

A prologue is optional. Its sole intention is to intrigue the reader. It should be short and sweet, not exceeding four or five manuscript pages, and should set forth why you are qualified to deliver the information.

In the prologue to Thomas Stanley's best-seller *The Millionaire Next Door,* Tom surprises the reader with the declaration that wealthy people are not the extraordinary and gifted human beings we think they are. He follows this with an insight into the actions affluent people take to accumulate such wealth. In the last part of the introduction, he establishes himself and his partner, William Danko, as experts by demonstrating the comprehensive research they have undertaken. If a potential reader interested in accumulating wealth were to pick up the book and start reading the prologue, he or she would feel compelled to read this book.

STEP 2—THE OPENING CHAPTER

This chapter should establish the main point of the book and tell readers what they will learn. Make a compelling promise to deliver "the goods"; for example, "By following the steps in this book, you will have a marketing system that explains your service or business."

Your book should start by establishing your credentials. If you're the head of an association or have a certification or distinction, are a Ph.D., or have been in the industry 20 years—whatever it is, early on you want to make sure the reader understands your background and your credentials. Sometimes credentials can be nothing more than a subject so deeply intertwined in your life that you can't write about anything else. After you have done your research and struggled to find the right words to make the best of your talent in the service of your subject, you earn the right to be its author.

STEP 3—LAY OUT THE PROBLEMS

Discuss the key concepts of your type of business or service—how to enhance your success, for example—that set the premise for the issue(s) or problem(s) you present. Lay out areas of concern and clearly state issues or problems. Talk about different risks. That will get readers starting to think. State the issue or problem you will resolve.

STEP 4—CURRENT TRENDS CHAPTER

You can help the reader understand how your service works. Cover three or four examples that show how different products work with each other. Discuss new strategies and why they work in this new economic environment. Use charts, graphs, and backup material. Use quotations from a recognized authority.

Look at current trends, and discuss why you think these trends will continue or correct. Rethink past advice and explain why it doesn't work today.

STEP 5—THE SOLUTION

Answer the original question you set up in the introduction or first chapter. Give readers solid proof that your system works. Follow this with a paragraph explaining how to put these principles to work. Talk about reasons for measuring and monitoring and how these keep you on track. State the premise of your solution.

STEP 6—STEPS AND TOOLS

Change the pace here and give some technical backup material. Perhaps present a selection of different service providers with phone numbers. Explain how to select one over another.

Show readers how to solve the main problem on their own. Walk them through a logical thought process (six or seven steps). Tools could include formulas, decision trees, flowcharts, case studies, checklists, and practice aids.

STEP 7—SUMMARY

Summarize your book here. Pull it all together. Condense all the information you gave readers in the previous chapters but in a format that helps them get started *now.* You want readers to feel a sense of the story coming to a successful and inspiring closure.

Don't forget to create a pathway to your product or service. Basically, use your book as a means to get more exposure, to get your name out in the world.

Glossary

Toss in a glossary of industry terms and list where you got your information—and you're done.

Appendix

I put the technical stuff here—mathematical formulas, studies, and the like.

About the Author

Tell your readers who you are, highlighting your qualifications, education, background, company, and position. Include a photo. I always let readers know how to contact me. A good place for contact information is on the inside back cover of your book.

Sample Bio

Larry Chambers is a freelance writer, a speaker, and a communications coach. His unique approach involves coaching people how to write for publication and place their own material. His clients have been published by major publishing houses, including Dearborn, McGraw-Hill, Random House, Times Mirror, Dow Jones, and John Wiley, as well as featured in major national trade magazines. Phone: 805-640-0888; Web site: <BOOKBOOTCAMP.COM>; E-mail: Lchamb007@aol.com

---

Testimonials

Include testimonials from your clients who are big hitters in their field. Before long, you will be perceived as *the* expert in your field. Your seminar is specific, your book is specific, your marketing is specific, and your life is simple.

HOW TO PREPARE A PROFESSIONAL MANUSCRIPT

Following are tips on preparing a neat, professional-looking manuscript. Begin with the correct paper—at least 16- or 25-pound quality. I submit by both hard copy and e-mail. I use a Hewlett Packard Laser Jet V printer, so every copy is an original. If you're using a typewriter, make sure that you always use black ink. Editors read numerous manuscripts weekly and don't appreciate eyestrain. If they come across something that has faded from sitting on a windowsill in the sunlight, they will chuck it.

Use a 12-point Courier typeface. Don't use fancy fonts. Editors don't want to have to decipher hieroglyphics. A dot matrix printer is also a no-no. The print should be as close to letter quality as possible.

Proper formatting will make it easier for the editor to typeset and the art department to lay out your manuscript. Leave a 1¼ to 1½ margin around the text. Use double-spacing throughout your story to permit easier reading and room for editing.

In the upper left-hand corner of the first page, type your name, address, phone number, e-mail address, and Social Security number. If the editor decides to use your manuscript and needs to get in touch with you immediately to verify information, your contact information is handy. On the upper right-hand corner of the first page, provide the number of words. Number every page.

Center your manuscript title on the middle of the page. Skip two lines and type your name. At the upper left of the second page and subsequent pages, include a header with your last name, dash, and a short version of your manuscript title.

DON'TS

You look like an amateur when you:

- Use staples and don't number pages. Before you send the manuscript, recheck it and make sure all the pages are included. Today, a lot of my submissions are over the Internet or fax machines. Still, a majority of manuscripts and queries are delivered in paper form.
- Include copyright and serial right notices. Today's copyright laws no longer require writers to put a copyright notice on their work to protect it. Anything an author writes is automatically protected and need not be stated on the manuscript. Using a copyright sends a red flag shouting "novice."
- Have typos and grammatical mistakes. If you have more than one or two errors per page, you should retype the page.
- Don't use proper postage. Include a SASE (self-addressed stamped envelope) if you want your manuscript returned. I indicate on the bottom that it's not necessary. If you do send a SASE, make sure you include proper postage. Almost all editors need a hard copy at some point in the

submission process, so if you're submitting by e-mail, the editor will usually ask you for a hard copy later on. I send a copy on a disk, sometimes one by e-mail, and always a hard copy as well. Submit your books electronically only when asked to do so.

WHAT DO EDITORS REALLY WANT?

- *A professional manuscript* neatly typed, free of mechanical errors, and one that reflects good editing.
- Good writing with interesting beginnings and specific detail. Does it make sense?
- A problem/solution–driven manuscript that moves the article ahead. Do you provide solutions?
- Be concrete! Be clear! Be captivating!

Dynamic Sentence Structure

- Do your sentences have variety? Vividness? Clarity?
- Do they vary in length? Do they have a rhythm?
- Do they have contrasting detail? Revealing detail?
- Do they engage the reader?

Power Words: Nouns and Verbs

- Are your verbs active rather than passive? Do they convey action? Movement?
- Beware of variants of *had*.
- Are your nouns specific?
- Avoid using modifiers to prop up weak nouns and verbs. If you have to use an adjective or adverb, find a stronger noun or verb.

Language

- Is the language specific? Colorful? Visual?
- Does it appeal to your target reader? Is it appropriate to your industry?
- Are transitions smooth? Clear? Do they propel the reader along?
- Don't use jargon or clichés; they clutter up the prose.

Tone, Style, and Voice

- Do word choice and supporting detail add texture and mood to your article?
- Is tone consistent (ironic, tough, funny, formal, casual)? Is it right for intended reader? I use a formal tone when writing a financial-type article or chapter.
- Does the narrative voice have authority? Does it flow? Capture the reader's imagination?
- Are there any awkward shifts in tone, style, or voice? Is there overwriting? Underwriting?

Keys to Revision

- Watch for changes in point of view (pov) and tense.
- Cut unnecessary words to strengthen your story.
- Avoid wordiness and redundancies. Tighten prose.
- Avoid starting sentences with "It" and "There."
- Avoid too many *that's, where's, who's,* and similar contractions.

Use Anecdotes

A story-within-a-story is a way to:

- Show rather than tell to create immediate visual image.
- Dramatize the information you want to pass along.
- Simplify a difficult concept.
- Illustrate a theme.
- Deepen characterization.

WRITER'S BLOCK

"It was a dark and stormy . . ." No, "It was a *very* dark and stormy . . ." No, ". . . a *really* dark and stormy . . ." "It was *incredibly* dark and stormy . . ." No, no, no, no.

Good writers just write it; and when it's done, they go back and edit it. I have to admit that sometimes I can't figure out the next line to write; or worse yet, I can't seem to write the best-seller. I just finished three books that were published in 2000; I have been working on this one, but it's still not good enough. I'm never going to write the great American novel; I'm never going to be Ernest Hemingway! A rejection still sends me into a shame attack!

What is a shame attack? That's the debilitating feeling that usually occurs when you tell yourself, "I'm not good enough." Sometimes we cover it over with angry or aggressive actions or we self-medicate; but, for most of us, a shame attack stops us in our tracks and we become unproductive. "I can't do this; I'm on overload!" Beneath our veneer of proud accomplishments is low self-worth, which creates anxiety and the need to control what people think.

Luckily, I found that driving around the lake in my bass boat with my son, Logan, can pull me right out of the trance. Suddenly, the depression is gone and I haven't even caught a fish. Then I'm back writing. I guess that's what they call a real Zen experience. I'm there for the process, not the result. I've heard that the happiest people in the world are process oriented and the most miserable people in the world are goal oriented.

For myself and my writing, the more I move from being goal oriented to process oriented, the better. Now, if I get stuck, I refer to my outline and research material. There's always something there to start the ball rolling again!

■ ■ ■ ■

23

Promote Your Book

There are 50 things you can do to promote your book. I'm going to list them, and if you see one you like, you can stop and read it more closely:

1. Send signed copies to your clients/customers. The fact that you wrote a book makes your clients look good. Everybody wants to be associated with success.

2. Don't forget one of the most important marketing resources of all: your staff. Giving your books to your staff helps you train them. This helps everyone in your organization become aligned so that everyone is on the "same page." Your story becomes consistent in articles, books, and with the people you work with.

3. Write an article and send it to airline magazines. In-flight magazines are read by multiple travelers. Readers tend to be book buyers—college educated, global travelers, English-speaking men and women in their mid-40s with household incomes of over $100,000 who travel for both business and pleasure.

   A profile of the top five in-flight magazines with hints on how to get your books the coverage they deserve is found at the end of this chapter.

4. Send your book to book reviewers. Most major book trade publications review pre-publication. Slap a Post-it note on the cover of the book that says, "Look at Chapter 7" or "Here's an idea." Articles,

checklists, and summaries always include the author's name, book title, publisher, and price.

5. Mail your book to *Bottom Line/Personal,* Marc Myers, Executive Editor 203-625-5291, Boardroom, Inc., 55 Railroad Avenue, Greenwich, CT 06836-2614; 203-625-5900; fax: 203-861-7443; Web site: <www. Boardroom.com>; e-mail: webteam@boardroom.com. This 1.5 million-circulation newsletter can sell tons of books. Articles, checklists, and summaries always include author's name, credentials, book title, publisher, and price.

6. Go to the *LA Times* Festival of Books, c/o Book Review Author Committee, Times Mirror Square, Los Angeles, CA 90053; 1-800 LATIMES, ext. 7BOOK.

   Subscribe to *Book Marketing Update:* John Kremer 800-989-1400, ext. 423; fax: 610-284-3704.

7. Send your book to Michael Lamb, the host and producer of *Moneyroom,* who wants to interview authors and experts who can "help our listeners grow an existing home-based business or small business, or help them start a home-based operation."

   The best way to reach Lamb is to mail review copies or fax a pitch letter to: Michael Lamb, *Moneyroom,* 9642 Clubhouse Court, Wichita, KS 67226; 316-634-2645; fax: 316-634-6885; e-mail: michael@moneyroom .com; <www. moneyroom.com>.

8. *In Pursuit of Success Show* sells an average of 300 books per show, according to host Joe Hill. The hour-long show reaches South Georgia and North Florida on WYHI-AM and WVOJ-AM and focuses on anything related to achieving success—from finance, self-help, selling, and motivation to education and relationships. Send review copies with press kit and then follow up by phone. Contact: Joe Hill c/o Top of the Hill, PO Box 6148, Fernandina Beach, FL 32035; 904-321-1169; fax: 904-321-2872.

9. *Nolan @ Night* welcomes guests on all subjects. Radio America's syndicated *Nolan @ Night* will interview authors on topics "from soup to nuts." The show airs from 9:00 PM–12:00 AM weekdays; it features a lively format and a wide array of topics. You are interviewed by telephone.

   Send information to: Kim Nolan, Producer, Nolan @ Night, 6518 Yadkin Court, Alexandria, VA 22310; 713-924-0072

10. Andrea Kay writes *Ask Andrea* and hosts a career-related radio show on WKRC Cincinnati that doesn't do interviews but often cites books

on the air. Pitch her via mail or e-mail at: PO Box 6834, Cincinnati, OH 45206; 513-221-6222, e-mail: askandrea@fuse.net.

11. *CBS This Morning* is very receptive to books; it likes to have authors on air and interviews up to three each week. "The breakthrough factor is very tough," says producer Carol Story. "I look at everything, but if something gets 30 seconds or a minute, that's a lot of time. I actually look at the book first and I read a page.

    CBS This Morning, 524 West 57th Street, 7th Floor, New York, NY 10019, 212-975-2824; fax: 212-975-2115; Planning Producer: Carol Story, 212-975-4112. Best contact for books/authors.

12. Success and failure stories are among the favorites of Rhett Palmer's *Florida Show,* which airs twice daily on talk WAXE in Vero Beach, Florida. The audience is over 30 and evenly split between men and women. Palmer favors passionate authors and especially likes success and failure stories, celebrity interviews, and travel pieces. WAXE, PO Box 39, Vero Beach, FL 32961; 561-567-1055; fax: 561-595-0214.

13. Send a pitch letter to *People* magazine's Jamie Katz, senior editor for book reviews. Be sure to tell him why he should pay attention—and quickly. Says Katz: "Give me solid information, and do a good job of positioning the book, including what else this author wrote and when, who was especially interested in the book and why, whether it hit the best-seller list, why it's exciting, and what the media plan is." Books and authors are also the source for many of *People's* human interest stories, and many self-published authors have been featured in such articles.

    People, Time Life Building, Rockefeller Center, New York, NY 10020; 212-522-1212. Mr. Jamie Katz, Senior Editor in Charge of Book Reviews, 212-522-0021; fax: 212-522-10006.

14. Send books to Editor Jodie Green of *Working at Home,* who also does a monthly feature on useful office products. *Working at Home* is a quarterly that wants books containing practical information on every facet of setting up and running a home office. Executive Editor Marty Munson says the 300,000-circulation magazine wants solid tips on how to grow a business, pricing strategies, and negotiating and handling tax matters. "We're very benefit and solution oriented. If it's something every business person needs to know, we're interested in it," Munson says.

    The quarterly publishes book excerpts and runs four book reviews each issue, again looking for general, service-oriented business books.

Jodie Green, Editor, Working at Home, 733 Third Avenue, New York, NY 10017; 212-883-7100; fax: 212-949-7002.

15. Consider the possibility of workshops that could be developed to tie into the book.

16. Consider using the book as the basis for a community college, extension, or night school course. If you like teaching, modify your book proposal to become the syllabus and submit it with your résumé to local colleges.

17. Consideration should be given to whether this is going to be a series of books.

18. Send letters to the major review programs and build a kit that's likely to get a follow-up, such as a review copy of the book, a press kit, print run—anything highlighted—and maybe the promotional schedule and any innovative publicity plans. There should be a follow-up call to each of these.

19. Establish an author's tour. Develop an invitation and invite writers to hear and meet the author. Consider arranging with local book stores to do sales at these meetings.

20. Send books for review to the following: *Kirkus Reviews, Book List, New York Times Book Review, Washington Post Book World, San Francisco Chronicle Book Review, Los Angeles Times Book Review, New York News Day, Chicago Tribune Book, USA Today, New York Review of Books.*

    A cover letter or press release that contains the basic facts about the book should be sent with each book. These facts should include (1) what this book can do; (2) the significance of the book—the benefit it offers; (3) the intended audience—who the book will help; (4) a biography of the author—how the author is qualified; and (5) a list of the author's previous books.

    For special reviews, you might write a personal letter to accompany the review copy and also have the author autograph the review copy. Above all, follow up. Once getting a review, follow up with a thank-you letter and let the publication know what the response has been.

21. Offer to give a lecture at bookstores using your book as the text as opposed to a book signing. It's a good idea to invite some of your clients or people of influence to your lecture to add credibility. Offer attendees something to take away.

22. Make copies of the best reviews and include those in news releases.

23. Send copies of the major reviews to your key book-selling contacts.

Sample letter

March 10, 2001

Genevieve Stuttaford
Editor, Nonfiction
Publisher's Weekly
245 West 17th Street
New York, NY 10011

Dear Ms. Stuttaford,

Enclosed please find a copy of my book *The First-Time Investor.* I'd appreciate it if you'd consider it for review.

One interesting note. One store, 57th Street Borders, has ordered a thousand copies of this book for a series of talks I'll be giving for a bank in New York in September.

Warm regards,

Larry Chambers

24. Write a news release about the book—no more than one page double-spaced that focuses on the news value and benefit of the book, not its contents. Focus on one main benefit or idea. Keep it as simple as possible. Avoid making judgments about your own book unless you are quoting someone else.

    For important editors, attach a personal note to the news release. According to one newspaper editor, the glitzy press kits are the first to hit the trash. The news releases with a handwritten note tend to get read. A trade magazine editor has also noted, "I'd rather see a well-written release any day than all the fancy packages on Madison Avenue."

25. Set up a Web page.

Sample Reviewers Fact Sheet

Title: *The First-Time Investor*

Publication Date 1/99   ISBN 0-07-013070-1

Publisher: McGraw-Hill   Pages: 297

Price: $19.95

BLURB

There is so much confusion today around investing. It paralyzes most first-time investors so that they often don't even try to get started. *The First-Time Investor* shows readers that investing is a matter of correct investment behavior: start saving money now; turn debt into equity; evaluate future needs; have a strategy, focus, and discipline; seek unbiased help when appropriate; and teach your children how to invest. A recent study showed the profits that investors made were eight times more dependent on behavior than on investment choices. *The First-Time Investor* explains why there are no investment gurus. It gives the reader a step-by-step blueprint of how the market really works and how to get started safely and confidently.

"*The First-Time Investor* offers real-world investment applications in an understandable way."

Jack Canfield, *Chicken Soup for the Soul,*
#1 *New York Times* best-seller

TABLE OF CONTENTS
    Part I -   Know Your Outcomes—Take Action
    Part II -   How Does It All Work?
    Part III - Putting Advanced Strategies to Work
    Part IV -   Investing around the Tax Man

PUBLICITY PLANS
Republic National Bank has scheduled a ten-branch tour by the author in New York March 22 through March 26, 1999.

26. Find a specific tie-in to current news events. That is far more likely to attract the attention of an editor than a plain book announcement.

27. Consider a pitch letter, which would be personalized for the targeted media. It should plant a potential story idea in the editor's mind or a specific angle on the news for that publication. Sign the letter—make it as personal as possible. Include your biography, spiced with several interesting notes that humanize you as the author, such as what incidents or experiences led you to write the book. Again, people like to read about people.

28. There are approximately 1,500 national syndicated columnists; identify which ones would make sense for you to contact.

29. Volunteer to be an expert resource for all major publications.

30. Consider using various wire services.

31. Go to the local news bureau of the major publications. They are easier to work with.

32. Consider whether you should write an op-ed page article. Several people have used this effectively.

33. Consider whether you should distribute news releases via a PR service, such as PR News Wire or North American Precis Syndicate.

34. Consider sending through the syndication a camera-ready news or feature story. For approximately $1,000 per article, Metro Creative Graphics has had an article hit as many as 7,000 newspapers.

35. Consider putting notices about the book on the computer bulletin board.

36. Do radio interviews by telephone.

37. Consider offering free copies of the book to radio and TV shows. These copies are typically given away as a promotion for the interview or during the interview. As a result of this promotion, one author was interviewed on more than 50 shows, with some interviews lasting as long as an hour and a half. David Chilton, the author of *The Wealthy Barber*, sent 20 free copies to each major radio and TV show. In the accompanying letter, he told the stations to give the copies to the camera people, receptionists, hosts, and other employees. As he wrote in the letter, "I guarantee that once you read the book, you'll want me on the show," and he was right. As a result of those media appearances, his book became one of the top best-sellers for two years running.

38. Send information on the book to *Talkers,* a monthly newspaper for the news and talk radio industry.

39. Consider arranging TV talk show appearances. If you do TV interviews, design some visual aids or props that will help make the interview interesting. Also bring an index card with names and the title of the book typed on it so it can be flashed on the screen when you are talking, letting people know who you are, what the book is about, and how to purchase it.

40. Consider setting up interviews with local TV stations for practice as well as exposure. One author, with his first book and the help of PR, spent about $3,000 per city for his 26-city tour, but it was worth it. It put his book on the best-selling list. Contact the regional bureaus of the Associated Press and United Press International when you're going to be in one of their cities to get their day book calendar of events.

41. Work with one of the major book chains to ensure that the book is carried in every city you will be visiting.

42. Consider sending copies of the book to opinion makers. MegaTrend was sent to the chief executives of the 500 largest companies. As a result, the executives generated very effective word-of-mouth promotion for the book, which went on to be a best-seller. The most effective, influential print media are the *Wall Street Journal,* followed by *USA Today,* the *New York Times,* the *Washington Post,* and the *Los Angeles Times.*

43. Do at least five promotions a day, which requires five contacts a day. Publicity generates publicity (75 percent to 80 percent of all news is planted); persistence is what works.

44. Consider using the book jacket as a brochure and marketing piece for the book.

45. Consider developing a business card that's in essence a wallet-sized billboard for the book.

46. Consider whether an audiotape series should be made to go with the book.

47. Send your book to your college or university alumni magazine.

48. Do a school giveaway of your book to raise money.

49. Do a player of the week–sponsored trophy.

50. Always send a copy to your own trade association.

TOP FIVE IN-FLIGHT MAGAZINES

American Way, with a circulation of 325,000, publishes two issues each month. "We are looking for books with a broad appeal to a wide, literate readership," says Nancy Stevens, book contact and associate editor. Two reviews of nonfiction business books appear in the Executive Reading section. Familiarize yourself with the magazine by calling for a free sample copy. Send and pitch all submissions, even columns and features, to Nancy Stevens. Stevens can be reached between 9:00 AM and 5:00 PM central time. Never fax. Collections of short stories, fitness titles, and self-published books are welcome, but the magazine tends to steer clear of general how-to books. The magazine does not run excerpts.

> Book contact information:
> Nancy Stevens, Associate Editor, 817-967-1783; e-mail:
> nancy_stevens@amrcorp.com
> *American Way,* 4333 Amon Carter Boulevard, MD 5598, Ft. Worth, TX
> 76155; 817-967-1804; fax: 817-967-1571; e-mail: americanway
> @compuserve.com; <www.aa.com/away>.

Attaché (U.S. Airways), with a monthly circulation of 400,000, is considered the "hippest" of the in-flight magazines. Abigail Seymour, features editor and book contact, reviews all submissions. Call her during the afternoon. How-to books go straight to the slush pile. The magazine prefers that authors write original pieces. Approach Seymour not only with savvy but with original, exclusive ideas. Pitch authors and careers rather than individual books.

> Contact information:
> Abigail Seymour, Features Editor, 336-275-7714.
> *Attaché,* 1301 Carolina Street, Greensboro, NC 27401; 336-378-6065;
> fax: 336-378-8278; e-mail: attacheair@aol.com.

Continental (Continental Airlines) has a circulation of 385,000. Executive editor and book contact Ken Beaulieu (bo-lier) calls the publication "the business publication of the sky." The Reviews section runs five book reviews per issue. Many business books find print in the regular columns, such as *Profiting from IPOs and Small-Cap Stocks* (in Personal Finance). Send and pitch all books to Beaulieu, even for columns and features. Call to ensure your book made it safely. Business and general nonfiction books have the best chance of being excerpted, but it'll take a big-name writer for fiction to be purchased.

Book contact information:
Ken Beaulieu, Executive Editor, 617-867-8128; e-mail: beaulieuk @pohly.com
Continental magazine, 101 Huntington Avenue, 13th Floor, Boston, MA 02199; 617-424-7700; 617-424-8905; <www.pohlypartners.com>.

Hemispheres (United Airlines) is the wining and dining magazine of the air. This monthly magazine with a 500,000 circulation uses mostly cooking and beverage titles. Business books can find a home in columns such as *Strategic Brand Management* (in Executive Secrets) and *The Investor's Web Guide* (in Investing). Send and pitch all books, even for columns and features, to editor and book contact Randy Johnson. The best time to contact Johnson is during the second week of every month. Rather than calling, fax all general queries and media announcements.

Book contact information:
Randy Johnson, Editor; e-mail; ranjohns@hemispheresmagazine.com
Hemispheres, 1301 Carolina Street, Greensboro, NC 27401; 336-378-6065; fax: 336-378-8265; e-mail: hmsphrlet@aol.com; <www.hemispheresmagazine.com>.

Sky (Delta Airlines), with a circulation of 500,000, uses books in several different ways. *Sky* also believes in excerpts. Duncan Christy, the editorial director, says, "Excerpts give readers a better feeling of books than reviews do." Because Christy works from his home office, send and pitch all books, even for columns and features, to his assistant at the magazine, Kris Hudson. It's best to mail and fax Hudson all info and queries, so she can easily forward them to Christy. Delta has a special magazine for its shuttle called *Delta Shuttle Sheet,* which uses Boston-based, Washington-based, and New York City–based books. (Ask for a sample copy.)

Book contact information:
Duncan Christy, Editorial Director
Kris Hudson, Assistant
Sky, 1301 Carolina Street, Greensboro, NC 27401; 336-378-6065; fax: 336-274-2220; e-mail: skymag@aol.com; <www.delta-sky.com>.

24

Turn Your Expertise into a College Course

Why not teach a continuing education course at your local university or college? One of my students became one of the most popular teachers at the University of New Mexico. She also runs a successful business. How does she accomplish all this? She never gives up.

Lucinda Fairfield got the position by doing in-depth research into what courses were taught in other colleges around the country, and particularly what courses were popular in her own region. Next, she familiarized herself with the Division of Continuing Education at the local university.

She discovered the division had a limited number of students and was seeking to increase enrollment. Fairfield went back to the drawing board and designed classes that would complement the interests of the division. She prepared a preamble that demonstrated she understood the goals were to increase enrollment, bring in tuition, and increase community participation. She stated that she believed she could assist it and presented four or five different class ideas. The officials were impressed; their enthusiastic response: "Great! Let's get on with it!"

WHAT TO TEACH

A class may be a success in Denver but for whatever reason won't work in Albuquerque—or vice versa. You have to be willing to experiment, perhaps fail, and repeat a class more than one semester to give it time to catch on. Because one class doesn't work doesn't necessarily mean there's no interest in what you have to say. It may only mean that today people are simply in the mood for discussion of a certain type of topic.

HOW TO TEACH

Lucinda Fairfield shared her teaching outline, which is detailed next.

Overview

The first night of class consists of an overview of the material that will be covered. Then the students are asked to state their names, what they do for a living, and what their goals are for the class. Make a conscious effort to remember everybody's name and refer to each one by his or her first name. Class enrollment is normally between 12 and 25 students.

People usually come to class with insecurities about your topic, and they often feel intimidated. Once students discover that the other people in the room are much like them—a nurse, a computer techie, a teacher—they relax. The personal introduction session breaks the ice and puts everyone at ease, so they're better able to learn the material. Then Fairfield talks about herself— what she does for a living and what her goals and objectives are for the class. Then they begin the learning process.

Introduction

As an introduction to the class, start by telling the students a personal story.

At the beginning of Fairfield's career, she was proud of herself for having passed the securities test on the first try. In fact, she felt extremely smug, smart, and clever—that is, until she stepped into the professional world of finance. She then found that what she'd learn new one day was contradicted the next day. She became confused and unsure of herself. After a couple of weeks, she wasn't feeling so bright anymore but rather humble and overwhelmed by the amount of information. Three or four months later, at a securities dinner, a colleague who had been in the business many years asked how she was doing. Fairfield replied, "I feel like I have some kind of learning disability. Every day I feel even more overwhelmed than the day before." The seasoned professional slapped her on the back and said, "Don't worry, kid, the first 20 years are the hardest."

She shares this true story with students to let them know up front that the introductory class is not going to give them every single bit of information they'll ever need to be skillful. The class should be designed to help students discover where to get answers to questions and what resources to depend on. The story also gives them an inkling of just how much information there is in your world and starts them off with a realistic perspective.

Introduce New Concepts

In the first full class, begin by talking about basic strategies and concepts. Fairfield first describes the practical. The class then investigates ways to generate income: employment, savings accounts, CDs; ways to generate growth: business, real estate, collectibles, stocks; and ways to generate tax savings: pensions, profit-sharing plans, municipal bonds, estate planning, life insurance, and the like. At the conclusion of that class, Fairfield gives her students an assignment.

Each subsequent class examines a single topic; for instance, how a portfolio is divided between income, growth, and tax savings. She has students examine their own portfolios relative to risk. "I give my students a number of assignments, but I don't collect or grade them. The assignments are designed to help students become more aware of what they have done to date with their own money, whether they have consistently followed good plans, whether they have examined and kept within their risk tolerance ranges, what their return expectations are, and so on."

YOUR BENEFITS FROM TEACHING

What's in this for you? A move a little higher up the ladder is possible. The first requirement is a sincere desire to teach. The second is a commitment to prepare information in a way that's meaningful and understandable to students. The third is a willingness to put ego aside, to be sensitive and keenly aware of the needs of the students. For instance, when a student states, "I'm not understanding this," or asks, "Could you please explain that in another way?" it's important that the instructor not make a negative judgment of the student. Such questions indicate that the teacher needs to find another way to convey her message. Some instructors have the attitude, "Look how bright I am. Look at how much I know." The point is to not use esoteric phraseology to show off. If students aren't getting it, the teacher has failed them.

How Teaching Contributes to Your Business

Tuition includes one individual session with the instructor for portfolio evaluation and planning. On the first night of class, there's a calendar on the table of available dates and times for students to schedule a one-to-one half-hour meeting with Fairfield. In that session, she will answer any personal or private questions relating to a student's portfolio or the market in general. This meeting is private, confidential, and held in her closed office. In class itself, Fairfield does not give specific recommendations on mutual funds, on which way she thinks the market's going, or how she feels about CDs versus annuities. The personal 30 minutes can be used by students to explore these areas with Fairfield. If a student raises a hand in class and asks, "What do you think of Fidelity?" her answer is, "If you'd like to discuss that, here's the schedule. I'll give you 30 minutes. Classtime is not the time or place for me to give you my personal opinion."

Trust is built in the class environment that would ordinarily take months. It's been a successful means of building Fairfield's business. By the time students show up for a personal appointment, they've already had at least three contacts with Fairfield in the classroom. Out of 25 people, 70 to 75 percent make appointments.

Fairfield's rating was very high: 68%.

Outstanding Effort Brings Benefits

Fairfield was named instructor of the year for her division and was interviewed on TV and radio. Now people recognize her on the street and identify her as an expert in the field.

There have, in fact, been many side benefits. "Two years ago, when Jazzercise Corporation was looking for someone to work with it, the university recommended Fairfield. Jazzercise asked how much she would charge. When she replied, "Six weeks, $5,000," the reply by Jazzercise was, "No problem," and she was on.

Jazzercise set it up—desks, chalkboard, everything. Fairfield taught the class twice to about 20 women each time. As a result, she was asked by an influential attendee to become a city sponsor, a very prestigious position. As city sponsor, Fairfield then gave a talk to 600 women about financial investing; it snowballed from there. These are just some of the spin-offs from teaching at the university.

There have been marketing advantages, too. The university pays for printing and sending out catalogs—about 50,000—containing her course description. It also takes care of the registration process and provides facilities. Fairfield picks up the list of students, shows up, and delivers. What could be better?

REVIEW

Steps to follow in proposing a course:

1. Research the school's philosophy, goals, and courses currently offered.
2. Compare its catalog with other college catalogs.
3. Write several course descriptions.
4. Find out who the decision maker is.
5. Get your materials together.
6. Send in your proposal or deliver it personally.
7. Follow up with a phone call.

It's important to remember that when a person undertakes teaching, the commitment is to teach, not to advertise. As soon as the message sounds like advertising, respect and attention are lost. You will be perceived by others as having a hidden agenda. The student is not there to hear about how wonderful the teacher is. The student is there to learn about your business, not to become your client or devotee.

STAGE FIVE

■ ■ ■ ■

STABILITY

Selective Retention

Your Message

Your Prospect

25

Putting It All Together

BUILDING A 24-MONTH CUSTOMER-CENTERED MARKETING PLAN

Firms that are successful invariably began with a written marketing plan. Large companies have plans with hundreds of pages; small companies can get by with a half-dozen sheets. Putting your marketing plan in writing crystallizes all those creative ideas you have floating around your brain about who will want what you have to offer, why, and how you plan to let them know about it. The main goal of your credibility-marketing plan is to *create the pathways that lead back to you, your company, or your service*. Focus on the practical, "sweat-and-calluses" areas of who, where, when, and how.

Don't confuse your marketing plan with your business plan. Your business plan spells out the purpose of your business—what you do and don't do, and what you want to do with it. Your credibility-marketing plan spells out how you bring in customers and keep them. Your company's business plan provides the environment in which your marketing plan must flourish; while your written marketing plan is your means to achieving the goals of your business plan. So, the two documents *must* work in concert.

Allow yourself a couple of weeks to write the plan, even if it's only a few pages long, and put it into a three-ring binder. Leave a tab for adding periodic reports; this will allow you to track performance as you follow the plan. Stick to your plan and refer to it at least quarterly—better yet, monthly. Commit to taking some action to move your plan ahead every day. Most marketing plans kick off with the first of the year, but you don't have to wait until then to install your plan. Don't fall into the trap of getting lost in the running of your business without taking the necessary steps to build the business you really want.

Before you begin to write, pull together some information you'll need. Getting the information first avoids interruptions in the thinking and writing process. Have the following on hand:

- Past marketing materials that have worked and/or failed
- Any scripts you've used in speeches or seminars
- Any reprints, articles, or books you may have authored
- A listing of each product or service in the current line, along with target markets
- A list of magazine editors or media people you know or *need to know*
- Copies of your clients' trade magazines or journals
- An organization table (If you can count your employees on one hand, you can probably omit this.)
- Your company's latest financial reports and historical sales figures by product and region
- Notes of your marketplace research: your competitors, geographical boundaries, types of customers you sell to, existing distribution channels, latest and most useful demographic data, and any information on trends in your markets (both demographic and product-related)

Market Research

Conduct extensive research. No matter what your company's size, get feedback from all aspects of your business—from your own key employees to suppliers, from other industry professionals to the competition. My experience is that most people are quite willing to share their knowledge, experience, opinions, and concerns. This research can provide invaluable insights about your market and how what you offer is perceived by your market. It could have a huge effect on the way you market yourself and your services. Ask the following questions:

- Are there any trends that are ominous? Favorable?
- Are your current products poised to succeed in the market as it now exists? In the future?

- What percentage share of your market do you command? How does that compare to your competitors?
- Are the demographics of your market in your favor? Against you?

Consider each of your products or services against the matching products or services of your competitors. How well do you stack up? Is there any significant market opportunity for you that neither you nor your competitors are currently exploiting?

You should always be in touch with the needs and desires of your prospective customers, what motivates them, and what challenges/problems they share in common. Conduct one-on-one interviews guided by a small checklist and basic common sense. Don't forget to ask your customers what they read and how they wish to be contacted.

Market Position

This section should contain your best and most clear-headed description of the current state of the marketplace (this is no place for hunches):

- What are your products/services?
- What is the dollar size of your markets?
- What is your sales and distribution setup?
- What geographic area do you sell to?
- Describe your audience in terms of population, demographics, income levels, and so on.
- What competitors exist in this marketplace?
- What is your historical success?

Much of this information exists in your head, but now is your opportunity to write it down. For example, how much information do you have in your office—right now—on your competition? A marketing plan gives you a chance to pull all this relevant information together in one place, to spur ideas, and to justify actions.

Marketing Objectives

Paint your picture of the future: What marketing objectives do you want to achieve over the course of the plan? These objectives should include both a narrative description of what you intend to accomplish, along with numbers to give you something concrete to aim for. Each marketing objective should have several goals (subsets of objectives) and tactics for achieving those goals.

Review your past sales numbers, your growth over the years in different markets, the size of typical new customers, and how new product introductions have fared. For instance, if over the past five years you've grown a cumulative 80 percent in gross revenues, projecting a 20 percent increase in the next year is reasonable; 50 percent is not. Make a low but reasonable projection for what you'll be able to accomplish with marketing support toward your new marketing objectives.

Keep your objectives challenging, yet achievable. Better to motivate yourself with ambitious, worthy targets than to depress yourself by failing at too many enthusiastic goals. Here are some typical marketing objective categories:

- Introduce new products.
- Move from commission to fee-only business.
- Extend or regain market for existing product.
- Enter a new market.
- Cross-sell one product with another.
- Enter into long-term contracts with desirable clients.
- Raise prices without cutting into sales figures.
- Refine service or product.

This section of your plan should include objectives with specific goals. Some examples:

- By the end of the year, we want to have one additional client with billed time of $95,000.
- Introduce a book boot camp by June 1.
- Introduce TV feature to services.
- Add large eastern institute as client.

The key task is to take each objective and lay out the steps you intend to take to reach it. As an example, let's take the first marketing objective mentioned. How can you make this happen?

Time frame. Your plan must address two different time frames: the short term (1 to 12 months) and the long term (over 12 months). Most of your document should focus on the coming year, which is the most important for the majority of small and medium-size businesses. Marketing typically demands the performance of a number of short-term actions planned in unison, which together bring about change. Once you've outlined the major year-end goals, the analysis will largely focus on the mechanics of media, mailing, and promotion. But you shouldn't stop your serious thinking at year-end. Stretch beyond your business's immediate needs and envision the next two or three years. What are you ultimately reaching for?

Budgets. Your marketing plan needs to have a section in which you allocate budgets for each activity planned. This information shouldn't appear on the activity matrix, because there's enough detail there already. But it should be in writing with the individual carrying overall program responsibility. People responsible for portions of the marketing activity should know exactly what funds are available to them.

Be as objective as you can about those costs you can anticipate. For things with which you have no budget experience, add 25 percent to your best estimate. Your budget should allocate separate accounting for internal hours (staff time) and external costs (out-of-pocket expenses).

Your budget section might look like this:

Gross sales	$500,000
Budget for annual marketing efforts	40,000
Internet site	3,000
Reprint letter mailing to prospects	600
Clerical help on mailing list	400
Advertising in trade magazine	500
Article reprints (brochures)	3,500
Editing	1,500
Printing	500
Registration for business exhibitions	500
Attend business exhibitions	3,000
Booklet writing project	25,000

Assign responsibility. Who's going to be in charge of each project? One of the best ways to handle such details is through an activity matrix. A matrix is a grid table that lets you plot actions across time. When you're developing a marketing plan, you'll soon reach the point where you have to turn to your calendar and see when things should happen. A matrix provides you with a clear and very usable framework for such timeline plotting. You can make the matrix as detailed or as "big picture" as you want.

Controls: Tracking effectiveness. *If you can't measure it, you can't improve it.* How will you make adjustments to your plan midstream? How will you monitor progress in sales/costs to make changes during the year?

Set up systematic reviews of your marketing strategies. Conduct a major review to track your progress at least every six months. This will create momentum, strengthen your vision, emphasize successes and achieved goals, and help you to stay on your marketing track. The reason you pick measurable marketing objectives is to have the ability to track your progress toward reaching them. Too many marketing efforts aren't quantifiable, with the result that the achievements of your marketing campaigns aren't satisfactory, or they're just plain illusory.

All your marketing efforts will benefit from the classic *feedback loop:* Act, observe, adjust, and act again. Scheduling quarterly meetings is best. At these meetings, responsible individuals should report on what they've accomplished in the last quarter, including how much of the budget has been spent.

As your activities move forward over time, you'll doubtless find the need to adjust the timing, the budget, the tasks themselves, or the people responsible. At these points, you must decide whether to intensify your efforts, add more tactical steps to pick up the pace, or scale back your objectives. Make your changes in an organized manner, adjusting all the dependent tasks so that the plan shifts as a whole. Whatever your decision, make sure to update your marketing plan document. Keep the original and date and number all changes.

Your plan must be dynamic, but it shouldn't lose its sense of history. Put in writing your understanding of why you didn't reach your goals. All this information will be extremely useful when you create next year's marketing plan.

Your effectiveness section might look like this:

1. Annual gross fees from the previous year $500,000
2. Actual marketing expenses last year   22,500
3. Anticipated impact of marketing expenditures on
   additional gross sales   125,000
4. Marketing expenditures planned during the current year   40,000
5. Annual gross sales at the end of the current year   925,000
6. Percentage of the actual difference between this year's
   sales and last year's sales that can be fairly attributed to
   the marketing effort   25%

Continually ask yourself these questions:

- Where can I make my market program stronger? What more can I do?
- Is my approach achieving the results I want?
- What parts of my business do I need to strengthen?
- How can I create more demand for my services and products?
- Who are the additional clients I really want?
- What do these preferred clients really want? What are their key current financial concerns?

Media Opportunities

When you're satisfied that your research reflects both the bad and good implications of the current market, identify media opportunities associated with those conditions.

Look for problems common to individuals within your target markets and develop solutions to those specific problems. For instance, companies that are downsizing could benefit from lump-sum distributions. Become an expert on lump-sum distributions if that is a prevalent concern, and then write about your findings.

Does your target market receive a specialized newsletter or publication? Would the director or editor of that publication print an article from you addressing the needs of readers? He or she would most likely be delighted. Call the publication and get the criteria for articles by outside authors.

Look for opportunities within your own client base. The top ten clients of most service businesses represent between 70 percent and 90 percent of total revenue. Therefore, if you could simply duplicate your top clients, you could more than double your net income!

Deliver Your Compelling Message Consistently

Communicate the right message to the right people at the right time through the right channels to be effective. Studies show that it takes about seven communication impressions to turn a prospect into a client. It takes time to gain trust, especially when major decisions are to be made. For optimal results, combine as many different types of communication as possible for each prospect. These can include direct mailings, trade association speeches or news articles, endorsements from centers of influence, workshops, and telephone follow-ups.

Make a commitment to *regularly produce communication pieces.* Don't make the common mistake of attempting to reach widely different markets or trade groups. Stick with one or two target markets. By focusing your thinking on a small and specific market, you will create tremendous growth in your business.

Send out reprints of relevant articles by you and other authors to clients and prospects. Reprints can act as calling cards and reinforce each level of your marketing campaign, positioning you as an effective advisor in the community you want to reach.

Join trade or professional associations in your target market. Because associations publish specialized trade magazines and newsletters, they are an effective way to keep track of news, people, trends, and up-and-coming events. Attend conventions, trade shows, seminars, and other networking meetings. Exhibiting at trade shows gets you deeply involved in a target market's community. You become one of them. People always prefer to do business with a person they know and trust.

Let people know you appreciate their business. Send them advance notices of seminars. A newsletter can keep your customers up-to-date. Test the letters you send out; test your copy. Follow up with a phone call. Verify results and assumptions. Whatever you do, don't give established customers a chance to forget or replace you.

Executive Summary

Put a brief summary at the front of your marketing plan binder. On a single page, sum up (with key financial numbers) the contents of your marketing plan. Use bullet points, short sentences, and bold type for major points, and stay focused on the big issues. What does someone have to know about your plan to get a sense of it?

This summary gives plan readers a concise description of what your company plans to do in the coming year. It also forces you to boil down your thoughts to their rich and flavorful essence.

Here's a sample marketing plan executive summary:

The year 2002 marketing plan for Chambers and Associates has four main elements:

1. Maintain position in market.

2. Review existing competitive marketing situation. Overall, prospects look good for our company. No competitive firm has made significant marketing efforts.
3. Market aggressively in the coming year. In addition to speaking and training engagements, prepare a series of three articles to run in late summer and early fall in trade magazines. Produce first company brochure for use as a handout at the training venues. Budget for production of the ads and brochure will be $4,500.
4. In the long term, explore the possibilities of doing a joint venture for a book boot camp. Toward the end of that period, hire at least one additional employee.

Identify both your short-term (next 12 months) and long-term (next 24 months) goals, rather than merely focusing on short-term sales results. Ideally, your short-term and long-term efforts mesh in such a way that each contributes to the other.

IMPLEMENTING YOUR MARKETING PLAN

Decide on a minimum period (I suggest 24 months) for implementing and testing your program. You must allow time for the constant improvement necessary to make your plan hugely successful. Things change, people leave, markets evolve, and customers come and go. Very seldom is the formula right in the first attempt; refinement through experience will bring success. If done well, your marketing efforts will become easier and better as the years go on.

Following are the stages of developing a credibility-marketing plan over 24 months and beyond.

Formulation: Days 1 to 10

Decide on the outcome you desire; plan/gather information/decide; take small steps and complete them; lower your expectations; determine what you need; decide the results you expect; set time frames; prioritize. Do first things first.

This stage gives form to your idea and helps you devise a plan for the type of project you want to generate.

Concentration: Days 10 to 30

Put your plan into action; box yourself in; gather more information; conduct research; tighten discipline; concentrate your attention; design a budget; produce a result.

You make clear-cut, simple statements of short-term results you want to produce. Your attention is concentrated; you are intense. You keep going no matter what, and you take no unnecessary outside actions. You are bold. The theme during concentration is to prepare to produce results. At this stage, there's high input, low output; ten in, one out.

Momentum: Day 30 to 6 Months

Keep doing what is working; elevate the level of communications; develop or add new strategies; conduct intentional campaigns to promote your project and create demand; discover the appropriate statistics; create a process for moving on to the next stage; put in what's missing; don't fix what's working.

Sometimes it's difficult to know when you've moved into *momentum,* but by studying the appropriate statistics for each phase of your project, you can track progress.

During this stage, you're going to experience a release of energy—maybe even spontaneity and inspiration. In other words, you'll have a very high level of activity. You may even start to enjoy the process of selling your products or services. The best salespeople don't sell—they *let* their customers buy from them.

At this point, you may want to expand or form strategic alliances or hire additional staff. There will now be more need for effective communications. It's also time to clean up the "wounds" left over from concentration and publicly communicate the vision of your business. You create more work, but not necessarily harder work.

To keep track of my projects, I designed a large display board covered with fabric. I made it fun by using small toy tanks to represent each project I was working on. I had markers to represent the number of pages needed for each project and lined the toys up at the end of the table. As I completed a day's work, I moved appropriate toys in the direction of the next stage of the process. I could visually see where all my projects were and how many pages were still needed to accomplish each job. It worked for me!

High Momentum: 6 Months to 1 Year

Find points of leverage; complete all loose ends; monitor your discipline; build strategic alliances; blueprint your business.

During the operating state of *high momentum,* rather than trying to handle everything, look for points of leverage. At this stage, concentrate on differentiating yourself from everyone else in your field. You're looking for what you can do that will really make a difference in your marketing. Complete all loose ends. Continue with your statistics project and monitor discipline so that you don't start to slack off. Add new phases of credibility marketing and/or people. Everyone involved should be concerned with the accomplishment of each complete project, rather than just producing a result or following an instruction.

Do what needs to be done, no matter what. This is one of the most difficult stages, because it may appear that everything is already running smoothly. Check and recheck.

Expansion: 1 Year to 2 Years

A sudden, sharp, steep rise in results: it's what you do when the breakthrough comes that is the subject of this chapter. Lots of action; patience; unreasonableness.

Expansion is unique in that it involves all other operating stages. Every time your project expands, you need to modify the established structure or create a new one that can evolve. The structure comes from reentering lower operating stages and moving through them.

Stability: 2 Years and Beyond

Consistently produce results; learn to measure so that the statistics are clear and sufficient; put in the "levers and dials" of your business; watch for the pitfall of boredom. Stability is a predictable result.

Stability can be a very difficult time for a new project or business. Stability should not consist of defensive strategy; it's an active stage, not a time to rest. It's a period during which you need to build up surpluses and reserves.

Everything is now basically in position, and the structure of your credibility marketing project is present and working. Short-term goals are understood; results are being accomplished; systems for monitoring the business are being utilized; expected results are being accomplished. Accountability is clear-cut; measurements and statistics are in place; sufficient leverage is being used. In short, everything that makes a successful business is pretty much in place.

Stability, however, can also be a dangerous time. It is the time when many people tend to relax and party. It's easy to become bored or too lax, if you don't realize the pitfalls present in stability. It's a common occurrence at this stage to slip back into a lower operating state, and even go into the danger zone by assuming you can just cruise now.

It's easy to become complacent; that's when a project can too easily slip into danger, or when you can lose a client by not taking enough of an interest. Another danger of complacency is of disengaging yourself from the rest of the world, business associates, friends, and family. Keep in touch with established contacts and make sure you're completely up-to-date with what's happening around you.

MASTERY

Most people think of expertise as an end point, but it's not. It's about process, not perfection. Mastery is defined as the state or condition of having power, control, or full knowledge of a subject.

Staying in the operating stages with full concentration on one's present stage allows access to this state. Mastery as an operating state is really about deepening your focus and letting go of worry, doubt, and future concerns. The overall objective of the operating states, in fact, is to take your concentration out of emotion that dissipates energy and focus on something tangible.

SYNCHRONICITY

How do you know when synchronicity occurs during an operating stage of your credibility-marketing program? Synchronicity is the coincidence of two or more events that seem to be linked in a meaningful or significant way without apparently being causally related. This normally happens in about the third year, but it can happen at any time. It's the adventure. If you have the courage to follow your dream, to take the risk, life opens up all along the line; doors open that weren't even there; there's a new sense of destined serendipity. It's not spiritual magic. As you look back, unexpected events seem almost as orderly as in a well-composed novel or like accidental meetings and turns in the road that seemed to have been mistakes at the time. Helpmates come along frequently to give you clues. Life seems as though it were planned beforehand. Mythology tells us that where we stumble is where our treasure lies.

I've known many people who have met someone new or reconnected with someone from the past, and that person unexpectedly becomes the conduit through which their publishing and marketing projects take off. Something happens here, and the result is realized over there. While each person and event *seems* separate and independent, seemingly unconnected events do influence each other in a myriad of ways.

26

Summation

Let's look at what we've accomplished in this book. I've given you enough information to get started on a credibility-marketing program that can help you build your business dramatically. The program is a three-year campaign. If you start today, three years from now you should have accomplished all the tasks, including writing a book.

In the beginning of this book, I said I was going to help you become a recognized expert using credibility marketing. I addressed the need to stand out and why you should want to be an expert. Being perceived as an expert creates an endless stream of prequalified, pre-endorsed prospects. I can tell you honestly, this program works.

Writing a book will help you get your thoughts organized, but the main benefit is gaining credibility. Clients will seek you out as the expert, the problem solver. You'll help them with their challenges and make solutions happen. You'll attract new clients, and your existing clients will perceive you differently. How many of you have seriously looked at your clients' problems and written out the answers? In that process, you start becoming the expert. It's a self-fulfilling prophecy—you *do* become the expert.

When you're perceived as the expert, your clients become your marketing apostles. You have impressed them, and they know that you deliver the goods. And this perception shortens the sales process. It tightens your business-planning process so you can be even more effective in meeting clients' needs, and it helps you make your business even stronger.

So what have you learned? How to position yourself as a media source; how to build a top-of-the-mind awareness system, which means when the media thinks of your profession, you immediately come to mind; where to find the media; how to write a how-to article and get it published; how to leverage your articles into books and brochures; how to write a query letter and a book proposal; how to use your articles and books to help prepare speeches, teach a college course, create an endless stream of prequalified prospects, and reinforce relationships with existing clients; how to build image and credibility; and last, how to shorten the sales process. Not bad for a day's work!

■ ■ ■ ■

Appendix A
Schedule of Fees and Costs

Ghostwriting Schedule of Fees and Costs

- Ghostwriting professional and trade journal articles under someone else's byline $1,500–$6,000

- Permission fees to publishers to reprint articles or stories $75–$500

- Copyediting $20–$50/hour

- Editing, general $500/day

- Fact checking $20–$50/hour

- Writing a financial presentation for a corporation—20–30 minutes $1,500–$4,500

- Ghostwriting in general $25–$200/hour

- Ghostwriting a corporate book, 6 months' work $20,000–$50,000

- Newsletter editing
  Some writers charge on a regular or monthly basis $50–$500 per issue, $25–$150 per published page

- Newsletter ghostwriting $800

- Article query letter $250/letter

- Book query letter $250/letter to publisher

- Outline of book $500/$1,000 outline

- Book proposal $2,500–$25,000/ proposal

- Copyediting
  Rates are generally at higher end of scale for reference material $35/hour, $6/1,000 words, or $2/page

- Ghostwriting a business book as *told to* Full advance and 50% of royalties or $10,000–$50,000 plus research time for 200–300 page book

- Ghostwriting without *as told to* credit for clients who are either self-publishing or have no royalty publisher lined up $15,000–$50,000 plus expenses with one-fourth down payment; one-fourth when book is

- Proofreading
- Research for writers and book publishers

- Rewriting
  Some writers have combined ghostwriting
  and rewriting short-term jobs for which
  they get paid $350/day and up; some
  participate in royalties for book rewrites
- Book summaries for business people,
  4–8 pages
- Business letters (such as form letters to
  improve customer relations)

- Business meeting guide and brochure
- Business plan

- Business writing on local or national level
  —advertising copy, collateral materials,
  public relations, or other
- Book proposal consultation

- Sales letter for business or industry

- Service brochure

- Trade journal ad copy
- Radio advertising copy
- Press kit
- Press release, 1–3 pages

finished; one-fourth at
three-quarter mark; and
one-fourth when
manuscript completed,
or you can negotiate
chapter by chapter
$12–$25/hour and up
$40/hour and up;
$50–$500/per day and
all expenses; some quote
a flat fee of $300–$500
for a completed job,
$18–$50/hour;
Sometimes $5/page

$500–$1,000

$100/business letter
$500 up/form letter for
corporation
4 pages/$500
$2/word;
$200/manuscript page;
$500–$2,500/project
$25–$60/hour;
$200–$500/day plus
expenses
$20–$70/hour; flat rate
$500
$350–$1,000 for 1 or 2
pages
12–18 pages/$2,500–
$4,000
$250–$500
$500–$1,000/script
$500–$3,000
$500–$1,500

Appendix B
Seminar Worksheets

Create profiles of the ideal prospects for each service offered at the workshop. Develop a composite profile of the ideal prospect to attract to the workshop. Identify key media to create strategic alliances with.

Workshop Preparation
1. Determine ideal length of workshop.
2. Determine ideal workshop tuition.
3. Determine ideal workshop format.
4. Determine brainstorming format for lunch.
5. Determine if we should use PR.
6. Establish strategic alliances with key publication(s) to help market and position the workshops.
7. Finalize workshop agenda and speakers.
8. Identify workshop facility locations.
9. Develop workshop schedule.
10. Refine presentation outlines, handouts, and visual aids. (Get help from qualified consultant.)
11. Review presentation outlines and visual aids.
12. Make final changes to presentation.
13. Copy and assemble handout packages for workshop attendees.
14. Purchase and prepare nametags.
15. Contract with an audio recording company to record presentations.
16. Set date and location for seminar follow-up meeting to review and refine the entire process.

Workshop Marketing Preparation (to-do list)
1. Develop newspaper ad.
2. Develop phone scripts.
3. Develop phone invitation schedule.
4. Develop mailing schedule.
5. Write a confirmation letter.
6. Create map to workshop facilities.
7. Develop phone confirmation procedures and schedule.

8. Prepare invitations
9. Rewrite and redesign workshop invitation package.
10. Create an executive summary highlighting the benefits of attending the workshop.
11. Print invitations.

Communicate Our Message

- Precall invitees.
- Mail invitations.
- Phone prospects to invite to seminar.
- Mail confirmation letter with map.
- Phone participants the day before workshop to confirm attendance.

Workshop Presentations

- Present workshop.
- Rearrange seating at lunch.
- Ask participants to complete evaluation form and sell them on the benefits of the *"Shareholder Value Checkup."*
- Review workshop results and requests for appointments immediately after workshop.
- Follow up.
- Listen to recordings of presentations and make refinements and changes.
- Develop a standardized follow-up process for all presenters to follow.
- Develop a standardized follow-up communications process for each company or division.
- Use follow-up tracking form to create leads.
- Assign leads to appropriate individuals.
- Send thank-you notes to participants.
- Set "check-up" appointments.
- Meet with individuals who request appointments and complete data-gathering interviews.
- The project coordinator reviews each data form and prepares recommendations for using services of the presenters to maximize each company.

Full-Day Workshop Agenda

Time	Presenter/Activity	Topic
8:30 AM	Continental Breakfast	Networking
8:55 AM		Introduction
9:10 AM		
9:50 AM		
10:00 AM		
10:50 AM	**Break (15 minutes)**	Networking
11:05 AM		
11:45 AM		
11:55 AM		
12:35 PM		
12:45 PM	**LUNCH (1 hour 15 minutes)**	
2:00 PM		
2:40 PM		
2:50 PM		
3:30 PM		
3:40 PM		
3:55 PM	Conclusion	
4:30 PM	**Debriefing**	

Estimated Workshop Budget

Workshop Preparation	
Revise/Create 3 slide presentations for accounting services	$15,000
Recording	1,000
Workshop Marketing	
Public relations campaign	1,000
Develop camera-ready newspaper ad	1,500
Rewriting/updating direct response mailer	2,500
Printing (250×4=1,000-8 pg. letters w/env. @ $65 each)	650
Mailing costs (1,000 @ $2.90 each) 2,900	2,900
Letter shop services (1,000 @ $.25 each)	250
Phone calling (1,000×3=3,000 calls @ $1.00 each)	3,000
Total Marketing Hard Costs	11,800
Meeting Costs (320 attendees total, includes service charges)	
Handouts (320 at $5 each)	1,600
Room rental (8 @ $2.50 each)	2,000
Continental breakfasts (320 @ $20.00 each)	6,400
Lunches (320 @ $40 each—includes speakers)	12,800
	(continued)

Refreshments ($600 per workshop)	$ 4,800
Audio-Visual equipment ($250 per workshop)	2,000
Total Meeting	29,600
Total Estimated Hard Costs	57,400
Unanticipated-Costs Cushion (× 10%)	+5,740
Total Estimated Budget	63,140
$7,893 per Workshop	

$1,579 estimated cost for each participating entity per workshop

Implementation Schedule

	Targeted Date	Completed Date	Assigned To
Target			
Evaluate expanding targeted companies	1/21/01	1/21/01	Mark
Create profiles of the ideal prospects	2/4/01		Mark
Develop a composite profile of ideal prospects	1/2/01		John
Identify key media	1/19/01		Marlene
Research			
Determine the best way to segment companies	1/21/01		John (interview)
Determine problems/opportunities.	1/21/01		John
Identify situations that prompt needs.	6/21/01		
Prioritize each niche			
Identify publications for alliances.			
Identify other promotional alliances.			
Packaging & Positioning			
Workshop Preparation			
Determine ideal length of workshop			
Determine ideal workshop tuition			
Determine ideal workshop format			
Determine brainstorming format for lunch			
Determine if we should use PR			
Create alliances with publication(s)			Larry
Finalize workshop agenda and speakers			
Identify workshop facility locations			
Develop workshop date scheduling			
Refine presentation materials			
Speakers review presentations (send)			
Make final changes to presentations			

	Targeted Date	Completed Date	Assigned To
Copy and assemble handout packages			
Purchase and prepare nametags			
Retain audio recording company			
Time/Date for Debriefing	Day of:	Day of:	

Workshop Marketing Preparation			
Develop phone scripts			
Develop phone invitation schedule			
Develop mailing schedule			
Write confirmation letter			
Create map to workshop facilities			
Develop phone procedures and schedule			
Utilize public relations			
Prepare Invitations			
Rewrite and redesign invitations			
Executive summary			
Print invitations			
Communicate Our Message			
Promotional Activities			
Precalls			
Mail invitations			
Phone prospects to invite to seminar			
Mail confirmation letter with map			
Confirm attendance			
Workshop Presentations			
Present workshop	Day of:		Team
Rearrange seating at lunch	Day of:		Hotel
Request appointments	Day of:		Team
Review workshop results	Day of:		Team
Review response sheets	Day of:		Team
Follow-Up			
Listen to recordings			
Develop follow-up process			
Develop communications process			
Create leads to follow up tracking form			
Send thank-you notes to participants			
Set "check-up" appointments			
Meet with prospects to gather data			
Send data to project coordinator			
Prepare recommendations for prospects			
Meet with prospects			
Ongoing communication			

Project Contacts

Firm	Responsibility	Phone

Firm	Responsibility	Phone

Speaker	Area of Responsibility	Phone

■ ■ ■ ■

Appendix C
Article-Writing Plan

The following outlines my understanding of our ARTICLE-WRITING PLAN going forward:

Goal is to have one major article published each month with others in the process of being published. There may be some overlap as we have no control over when the publishers will choose to print the submission.

THE THREE TARGET MARKETS

Could you expand your definition of the following markets:

1. Person(s) responsible for authoring article(s): _____

   _____

   Appropriate publications:

   _____

   _____

   _____

2. Person(s) responsible for authoring article(s): _____

   _____

   Appropriate publications:

   _____

   _____

ARTICLE GUIDELINES

The following is provided to help your staff with writing a commercial article:

How to Write Problem/Solution-Type Articles

Step 1. Identify a problem or concern your clients all share.
Step 2. Pose this problem as a question.
Step 3. Identify the compelling promise of your article.
Step 4. Title/Subtitle
Step 5. Identify three related problems that are a result of the main problem.
Step 6. Provide the solution to the main problem or problems.
Step 7. New discoveries—or charts
Step 8. Write about a personal experience.
Step 9. Call to action
Step 10. Summary

It's human nature to act from a desire to remove pain, to avoid loss, or to achieve gain. The internal message of any marketing communication is composed of those key items that are the most motivational to prospects (i.e., the *offer,* the *benefits,* the *time limit,* the *testimonial*).

Articles should be written to solve advisors' and/or their clients' problems. A good start would be a two- or three-page, approximately 500-word problem/solution process providing practical information to a targeted publication's readership on their specific interests. Don't waste words; no one wants details. People want benefits.

Lead with the strongest single benefit for that market. (Consider that a nationwide marketing study revealed brokers over 40 say they are primarily motivated to buy products, not because of the commission they receive, but rather by the way they are treated. Brokers under 40, however, were more interested in price and product issues and gave service a second place.)

Always *prove* every statement you make. Reinforce benefits with testimonials. It's a cynical world. You need third-party reviews, testimonials, reports, studies, confirmation of satisfied customers, third-party credibility marketing.

Prospects believe that most advisors would say anything to make a sale. Because this is a common belief among most American consumers, start from a different place. Assume your prospect will not believe you or trust you immediately, and then proceed accordingly.

- Include at least one problem followed by a solution.
- Never assert, always prove.
- Keep sentences short.
- Provide access for an immediate response (if desired).

WORKSHEET

Step 1—Identify a problem or concern your clients all share.

_____

_____

_____

_____

_____

_____

_____

Step 2—Pose this problem as a question.

_____

_____

_____

_____

_____

_____

_____

Step 3—What is the compelling promise of your article; what will the reader gain by reading your article?

_____

_____

_____

_____

_____

_____

Step 4—Title/Subtitle

_____

_____

_____

_____

_____

_____

Step 5—Identify three related problems that are a result of the main problem to give the article more depth and demonstrate a fuller understanding.

1)

_____

_____

_____

_____

2)

_____

_____

_____

_____

_____

3)

_____

_____

_____

_____

_____

Step 6—Now provide the solution to the main problems.

This is not intended to pitch your service or product but to provide the reader with the answer to the problem you described—possibly a series of steps.

_____

_____

_____

_____

_____

Step 7—Include new discoveries, studies, or charts.

Notes:

_____

_____

_____

If I were trying to show why investing in the latest fads don't work, I might include a chart.

Step 8—Write about a personal experience (optional).

Your personal experience establishes a strong initial connection between you and your readers. At its very simplest, you need to grab attention by relating a pertinent thought, insight, or observation that gets your main point across. Just use everyday experiences.

_____

_____

_____

_____

_____

_____

_____

Step 9—Include a *call to action*.

Example: For a copy of the research report, contact the author at _____.

_____

_____

_____

_____

_____

_____

_____

Step 10—Summary

Sum up your conclusion with information your reader can use. The more clearly and forcefully stated, the greater the likelihood that what you say will be remembered accurately. You could close with another colorful anecdote, this time one with a positive outcome that portrays an opportunity. It may include a "call to action," which is an alternate approach to telling your readers that they are now ready to act on what they have learned. I sometimes include a "quick-start" list, such as "Five things you can do to start your (   ) program."

_____

_____

_____

_____

_____

_____

_____

_____

Checklist
- Does the article have a clear story problem or question?
- Do the steps relate in some way to the story question or problem?
- Do the steps follow one another in logical order?
- Can you trim or eliminate anything without seriously damaging the content?
- Does your ending answer the question or problem?
- Can you think of anything more to include? Charts, graphs?
- Did you contrive an ending that leaves readers feeling they've learned something?
- Did you leave a way for readers to contact you?

Include your bio as a short verbal statement about who you are or what you do and a phone number and address.

Appendix D
Sample Book Proposal

1. List author(s) name, address, phone, fax, e-mail:
   Larry Chambers
   c/o Larry Chambers
   P.O. Box 1810, Ojai, CA 93024
   Phone: 805-640-0888; Fax: 805-640-0889
   lchamb007@aol.com

2. Title and subtitle of book: *First-Time Investors*

3. This book is primarily a general trade and professional reference. Soft-cover. Workbook 8½ by 11. 150–200 pages; tools and graphs; things people can get their hands on and use.

4. A short description of book: Workbook to get started. Easy and fun yet the book will reveal the same investment advice the affluent and super-rich receive and use. How readers can also use this information for their own investments.

5. Detailed summary of book: The paradox of life is that the greater your need for something, the less your chance of getting it. The psychiatrist who has years of experience and knowledge of how to treat chronic conditions doesn't have to deal with crazy people. Those patients are seen by interns. When someone is desperate for love, they repel those who might otherwise be attracted. And haven't you always heard that to get a bank loan, you have to prove you don't need the money? The same is true in the securities industry. Novice investors or those who can't afford to risk much and are really in need of advice usually end up with the most inexperienced advisor or fall prey to the latest investment trend.

   Today's investor has gone from being dependent and unknowledge-able to becoming interdependent—a combination of the investor un-derstanding how it all works and finding information online.

   From basic investing to advanced strategies, readers can apply this in-formation at their own pace, gaining confidence and the ability to avoid emotional investment decisions and to recognize misinformation in an ever-expanding, competitive marketplace of investment products.

This book will bring together concepts from other books into a single interactive whole. It will be designed to take anyone who can read (with no preexisting financial knowledge or interest) through a tour of how to get started and the right way to do it. The idea is to teach you to guide yourself.

The problem: Today's investors are faced with a level of complexity of investment decisions that have grown exponentially over the last decade. It follows, then, that one of the most important issues affecting investors today is how to find accurate and appropriate information necessary to make these decisions.

In addition, like a person trying to make up for lost time, most of us are drawn to the high returns touted by competitive investment products. But following high returns, without considering the amount of financial risk involved in achieving those returns, often proves disastrous. Investors must understand why risk is their friend and how it can be measured.

But risk is not bad. When you are behind, you do have to play catch up. I'll address that strategy and show readers Warren Buffett's approach.

Knowledge is power. From this workbook, readers can learn everything an astute investor, trader, or financial advisor must know before they commit to a plan. I'll examine various investment strategies and weed out those that have been proven ineffective. I'll discuss the characteristics of a successful investor as well as the traits that hinder one's chances for success. Readers will discover why the following four questions must be answered before starting an investment program:

1. What do you want your investments to do for you?
2. What is your current financial situation?
3. What is the level of risk you are willing to tolerate?
4. What is the time frame for achieving your investment goals?

The answers to these and other questions about an individual's financial personality will help that investor determine what to do to make the most of his or her money.

In the end, if you knew you ultimately couldn't lose, that there were no secrets, and that it could all be explained, wouldn't investing take on a whole new aspect? You wouldn't run out of patience or feel overwhelmed and give up and do nothing. You'd settle in and confidently wait for the inevitable gain to occur. You could stop focusing on trying to find the hot mutual fund and set about building your overall net worth—the ultimate goal of this workbook.

6. Key features that could be used in promoting the workbook:
   - Figuring out how much you have to invest
   - How to get started
   - Discovering which investment strategy is best for you
   - Uncovering the best sources of stock market information
   - Finding out how to buy stocks and funds online
   - How to set up a winning investment strategy from your checkbook
     Narrow your choices. With 45,000 mutual funds, there are too many choices, so narrow them down to a few.
7. The workbook's primary target market: general investing public along with taxable mutual fund investors and advisors.
8. Primary and secondary end users of book: everyday readers interested in understanding more about a frequent news topic and/or financial gain from investing.
9. Competitive books
10. Potential in the professional market: Professional societies, associations, firms' training programs, and/or other investment groups and organizations are likely to purchase this book in quantity. Likely to be included in professional books displayed at IAFP annual meeting.
11. Author's intentions for marketing the workbooks: to add credibility to business
12. Manuscript length: 195 pages
13. Completion date: six months
14. Authors' biographical sketch:

    Larry Chambers has authored and coached the writing of 30 books and over 700 magazine articles on the subject of investing. He writes for some of the top national investment advisors, who represent over $6 billion in managed assets, as well as for one of the nation's leading CPA firms. Chambers has been published by major publishing houses, including McGraw-Hill, Random House, Times Mirror, Dow Jones, and John Wiley; and he has been featured in hundreds of national investment trade magazines. In 1976, Chambers led the firm of EF Hutton & Company in managed accounts and was on the 1977 list of the top ten brokers in the nation.

15. Table of Contents:

Table of Contents

So many books on success begin something like this: There have been a great number of books written on the subject, many of them very helpful, but none have organized the principals into an easy-to-understand format.

Although I understand the accepted theme in today's celebrity self-help books has been "success," I've observed that many of them have not been helpful. In fact, most of them, including some of the more famous best-sellers, have been harmful to millions of readers who have blindly followed their advice. Most can't stand up to the realities of life. They simply tell the reader the way they would like it to be. This book is more about reality in investing, and I hope you will see and learn from a pattern in today's investing.

PART I: KNOW YOUR OUTCOME; TAKE ACTION

This Section Covers:

- Getting Started
- You and Investing
- How Do I Get Started?
- Informed or Wasting Time?
- Stock Market Investment Strategies
- How Do I Read All This Stuff?
- Get a Financial Coach
- How Much Money Is Enough?

PART II: HOW DOES IT ALL WORK?

This Section Covers:

- Understanding How Mutual Funds Work
- Types of Funds Explained
- Resources for Fund Information
- How to Read Newspaper Mutual Fund Tables
- Understanding Types of Stocks

- Understanding Types of Bonds
- Major Types of Mutual Funds
- How Does a Stock Exchange Operate?
- Locating Winning Funds and Individual Stocks

PART III: HOW TO PUT SIMPLE STRATEGIES TO WORK

This Section Covers:

- Warren Buffett's Investment Strategies
- Investment Architecture of Modern Portfolio Management
- Utilize Diversification Effectively to Reduce Risk
- Building Your Model Investment Portfolio
- Building the Asset Class Portfolio One Asset Class at a Time
- Step 1. The 60%–40% Investor
- Step 2. The Indexed Portfolio
- Step 3. Adding Global Funds
- Step 4. Putting It All Together
- Step 5. Rebalancing

PART IV: TAX-DEFERRED INVESTING

This Section Covers:

- How You Should Invest for Retirement Income
- The Power of Tax Deferral
- Financial Planning on the Web
- Retirement Plans
- IRAs
- The Roth IRA
- Retirement Plans for the Independent Business
- 401(k) or 403(b)?
- What Are Annuities?
- What Are Variable Annuities?
- Social Security: Good News to Save You Money!

PART V: HOUSE CLEANING

This Section Covers:

- Do-It-Yourself: Online Investing
- Where Do You Go for Online Help?
- Other Assets
- How to Select Your Investment Advisory Team
- How to Analyze an Investment
- How to Read a Prospectus
- How to Pay for College!
- The Regimen of Investing
- Changing Your Kids' Minds about Investing

Appendix E
Sample Article

state of mind

Bruce
Gladstone
Ph.D.

Tale of Adolescent Elephant Rampage Helps Understand Teen Violence

Tale of adolescent elephant rampage helps understand teen violence

One evening I watched a remarkable program on the Discovery Channel about the mysterious killings of numerous rhinoceros somewhere in Africa. Many rhinos had been found dead after being badly beaten and gorged. It was clearly not the work of poachers who used guns and who took the rhinos' horns.

These rhinos had been brutally beaten and mauled. Who could have done such a thing and why?

Animal experts investigating these unusual rhino killings soon learned that the killers were adolescent male elephants roaming in small bands. They filmed these bands of teen-age elephants chasing the rhinos, teasing them, throwing rocks and dust at them, pushing them down and preparing to gorge them with their tusks.

While the mystery of the rhino deaths was solved, the question still remained as to why the adolescent male elephants would behave in such an aggressive manner, so belligerent and out of control.

As the investigators continued to observe the teen-age elephants, they noticed that there were no mature male elephants around. They had all been poached for their tusks. The absence of mature adult male elephants was striking, but could it account for the murderous rampage of the teen-age males?

To find the answer to this question, the investigators arranged for several bull elephants to be imported to the area. Within a short period after the mature male elephants arrived, the killing and harassment of the rhinos by the bands of adolescent males stopped completely. The simple presence of the mature males

was enough to accomplish this result. When the male teen-agers stepped out of line and threatened the rhinos or overstepped their boundaries, a gesture and a bellow from the adult males brought them back in line. The young males even seemed to welcome the stability and authority of the older bulls.

In our society an increasing number of young males seem lost and out of control, as recent shootings in schools across the country indicate. Verbal abuse, belligerence, disrespect for elders and authority and a sense of hopelessness seem to go far beyond healthy adolescent rebellion in search of identity. My sense is that the shootings are just the "tip of the iceberg" of very serious problems for boys in our culture which we have not wanted to face. Hopefully we will begin to face them, quickly and thoughtfully.

At times, the behavior of many young males scares and intimidates us, as they mock our values, defy rules and identify with antisocial energy like fascism, racism, neo-Nazi and other hate groups. Often it seems there are no accepted rules, anything goes, everyone looks out only for himself, there are no accepted boundaries and no one is in charge. Of course, this is not true for all adolescents, but it is true enough to warrant grave concern from all of us.

Although the troubles of our youth today are much more complex than the troubles of adolescent elephants in Africa, there is no denying that father absence is a problem our teens have in common with the elephants.

In our industrialized and technological society, fathers have become increasingly absent from their homes and family life and from the responsibilities of raising children. This is one consequence of the Industrial Revolution, which began in the

1800s, and of our competitive, compulsive work ethic. Most fathers work long hours in industry, businesses and professions farther and farther from home. Technology has not made more time for parenting.

There are many ways fathers leave their sons. They are poached by a ruthless work ethic that insists on winning at all costs and making money as the highest forms of success. They leave through alcohol, drug abuse and television. They leave through marital strife and divorce. They exit through doors maintained by an educational-corporate-socio-economic system which declares that men should not feel.

As fathers have become increasingly absent, adolescent males have become increasingly agitated.

The focus of parenting (fathering) them is more on control, management and discipline and less on knowing them, connecting with their souls, uplifting and developing their unique gifts and creative genius. There isn't time for all that! Too often, the essence of who a boy is gets lost in the shuffle of working schedules, "busi-ness" and other priorities, until it is too late. Adolescent boys feel lonely, sad and abandoned in our society and they cannot admit to it. It's not their job to admit to it. That is our job, the job of their fathers and mothers, and it is time we all wake up to that and begin thinking of making some serious changes in how we raise boys to be men.

Like the rampaging adolescent elephants in Africa, our boys need strong, loving and mature male influence. They need their fathers and they need the entire village. They need to know who is in charge. They need to know what the rules are and they need firm, loving attention. Many boys get this, but far too many do not.

Source: *Ojai Valley News*, 14 May 1999. Used with permission.

Appendix F
Suggested Resources

American Society of Journalists and Authors, 212-997-0947. Founded in 1948, the society has a coast-to-coast and overseas membership of more than 800 independent freelance writers who have met ASJA's exacting standards of professional achievement. Call its Dial-A-Writer 212-393-1934 referral service. Fees are negotiated directly with the writer.

Editorial Freelance Association, New York, 212-929-5400. Web site: The-efa.org

Check online services such as *National Writer's Union* <www.nwu.org>, New York, 212-254-0279

Society of American Business Editors and Writers is headquartered at the School of Journalism, University of Missouri. Contact Executive Director Carolyn Guniss at 573-882-7862. The school can make an inquiry in the job section of its newsletter. If you are interested in writing a textbook, Ms. Guniss can hook you up with an academician at the School of Journalism: Sabew.org

Society of Professional Journalists, 765-653-3333.

Writer's Digest publishes each year a complete guide to writers' conferences, seminars, and workshops. Write or call for more information: *Writer's Digest,* 1507 Dana Avenue, Cincinnati, OH 45207; 513-531-2222; e-mail: writersdigest@fwpubs.com.

Writer's Market has a comprehensive listing of organizations by category and ethnicity.

Books

Bly, Robert W. *Targeted Public Relations.* New York: Henry Holt, 1993. How to get thousands of dollars of free publicity. Excellent book.

Boswell, John. *The Awful Truth about Publishing: Why They Always Reject Your Manuscript . . . and What You Can Do about It.* New York: Warner Books, 1986. A view from the other side—that is, the view from within the large publishing house.

Burgett, Gordon. *The Writer's Guide to Query Letters and Cover Letters.* Rocklin, Calif.: Prima, 1992. Sound and pointed advice from an expert's perspective on how to utilize query and cover letters to sell your writing.

Chambers, Larry. *The Guide to Financial Public Relations: How You Can Stand Out in the Midst of Competitive Clutter.* St. Lucie Press, 800-272-7737, Catalog #JM121; $49.95 each, plus $8.95 shipping/handling.

Collier, Oscar, with Frances Spatz Leighton. *How to Write and Sell Your First Nonfiction Book.* New York: St. Martin's, 1994. Practical, encouraging how-to from industry professionals. Topics include choosing a subject, targeting an audience, proposal writing, effective researching, conducting interviews, dealing with agents and editors, understanding contracts, and marketing your book.

Cool, Lisa Collier. *How to Write Irresistible Query Letters.* Cincinnati: Writer's Digest Books, 1987.

Curtis, Richard. *How to Be Your Own Literary Agent: The Business of Getting Your Book Published.* Boston: Houghton Mifflin, 1984. Insights and how-to; a personal point of view from one who knows the ropes.

Dustbooks (editors). *The Directory of Small Press Editors & Publishers; Directory of Poetry Publishers; The International Director of Little Magazines and Small Presses; Small Press Record of Books in Print.* Paradise, Calif.: Dustbooks, all volumes published annually. This set of literary references is put out by the publishers of the industry journal *Small Press Review.* These resources for market exploration also provide writers with editorial requirements and procedures for manuscript submission keyed to the individual publishers and periodicals listed.

Gage, Diane, and Marcia Coppess. *Get Published: 100 Top Magazine Editors Tell You How.* New York: Henry Holt, 1994.

Gladwell, Malcolm. *The Tipping Point, How Little Things Can Make a Big Difference.* New York: Little, Brown, 2001.

Godin, Seth. *Permission Marketing, Turning Strangers into Friends and Friends into Customers.* New York: Simon & Schuster, 1999.

Henry, Rene Jr. *Marketing Public Relations.* Ames, Iowa: Iowa State University Press, 1995. Tells the reader how to make it work.

Herman, Jeff, and Deborah M. Adams. *Write the Perfect Book Proposal: 10 Proposals That Sold and Why.* New York: John Wiley, 1993. Analysis of successful nonfiction book proposals with pointed commentary from New York literary agent Jeff Herman and book-proposal doctor (and author) Deborah Adams. Doesn't just tell you how to do it—this book shows you in detail how it was done.

Holmes, Marjorie. *How to Write and Sell Your Life Experiences.* Cincinnati: Writer's Digest Books, 1993.

Horowitz, Lois. *Knowing Where to Look: The Ultimate Guide to Research*. Cincinnati: Writer's Digest Books, 1984. An invaluable tool for anyone who has to dig up elusive facts and figures.

Kremer, John. *Book Publishing Resource Guide*. Fairfield, Iowa: Ad-Lib Publications, 1990. Comprehensive listings for book-marketing contracts and resources; contains a vast bibliography and references to other resource guides.

———. *101 Ways to Market Your Books—For Publishers and Authors*. Fairfield, Iowa: Ad-Lib Publications, 1986. Sensible, innovative, and inspiring advice for producing the most marketable book possible and marketing it as effectively as possible.

Larsen, Michael. *How to Write a Book Proposal*. Cincinnati: Writer's Digest Books, 1985. A clear and no-nonsense—even inspiring—step-by-step guide to the book proposal. The author is a West Coast–based literary agent and writer.

Luey, Beth. *Handbook for Academic Authors*. Rev. ed. New York: Cambridge University Press, 1990. This reference pinpoints key (and perhaps unsuspected) considerations in the field of academic publishing; valuable information with strategic implications for players in the publish-or-perish game.

Lyon, Elizabeth. *Non-Fiction Book Proposals Anybody Can Write*. Hillsboro, Oregon: Blue Heron Publishing, 1995.

Parinello, Al. *On the Air: How to Get on Radio and TV Talk Shows and What to Do When You Get There*. Hawthorne, N.J.: Career Press, 1991. Exciting guide to the electronic media and their use for promotional purposes. Ties in marketing aspects of seminars, social activism, and professional training and advancement. Especially appropriate for entrepreneurial authors.

Poynter, Dan, and Mindy Bingham. *Is There a Book Inside You? Writing Alone or with a Collaborator*, $14.95. Para Publishing, 1998. Also available in a six-cassette audio album. Also see <www.ParaPublishing.com>.

Preston, Elizabeth, Ingrid Monke, and Elizabeth Bickford. *Preparing Your Manuscript*. Boston: The Writer, 1992. Contemporary guide to manuscript preparation. Provides step-by-step advice for professional presentation of work for submission to editors, publishers, agents, and television producers. Covers punctuation, spelling, indexing; examples of proper formats for poetry, prose, plays; essential information on copyright, marketing, mailing manuscripts.

Sacharin, Ken. *Attention: How to Interrupt, Yell, Whisper, and Touch Consumers*, AD-WEEK BOOK 2000.

Shenk, David. *Data Smoke: Surviving the Information Glut.* New York: Harper-Collins, 1997.

The Writer Magazine, Cincinnati, Ohio (and newsstands).

Writer's Market. Cincinnati: Writer's Digest Books, published annually. A directory of thousands of markets and outlets; best known for its listing of the hundreds of consumer and trade periodicals. Also includes book publishers, book packagers, greeting-card publishers, syndicates, and more.

Magazine Writing

Digregorio, Charlotte. *Beginner's Guide to Writing and Selling Quality Features.* A simple course in freelancing for newspapers and magazines. $12.95. Civetta Press, P.O. Box 1043-P; Portland, OR 97207-1043; 503-228-6649.

McKinney, Don. *Magazine Writing that Sells,* $16.95. Cincinnati: Writer's Digest Books, 1994.

The Writer's Handbook. How and where to sell magazine articles, fillers, scripts, and book manuscripts. An anthology of helpful chapters with a lengthy directory of resources. $30.70 ppd. The Writer, 120 Boylston Street, Boston, MA 02116; 617-423-3157 or 888-273-8214; fax: 617-423-2168; e-mail: writer@user1.channel1.com; Web: <www.channel1.com/thewriter/>.

Wilson, John M. *Complete Guide to Magazine Article Writing,* $17.99. Cincinnati: Writer's Digest Books, 1993.

Yudkin, Marcia. *Freelance Writing for Magazines and Newspapers: Breaking In without Selling Out,* $11. (New York: HarperCollins, 1993).

Journal Writing

Shulman, Joel J. *How to Get Published in Business/Professional Journals,* $28.95. Jelmar Publishing Co., P.O. Box 488, Plainview, NY 11803; 516-822-6861.

Newsletter and Newspaper Writing and Publishing

Beach, Mark. *Newsletter Sourcebook,* 137 pages, $29.95. Cincinnati: Writer's Digest Books, 1998.

———. *Editing Your Newsletter,* $22.95. Cincinnati: Writer's Digest Books, 1995.

Brigham, Nancy. *How to Do Leaflets, Newsletters, and Newspapers,* $14.95. Cincinnati: Writer's Digest Books, 1991.

Dorsheimer, Wesley. *The Newsletter Handbook; How to Produce a Successful Newsletter,* 194 pages, $14.95. Hippocrene Books. 201-568-5194; 201-894-5406.

Hudson, Howard Penn. *Publishing Newsletters,* 224 pages, $39.95. H&M Publishing, 44 West Market Street, P.O. Box 3ll, Rhinebeck, NY 12572; 800-572-3451; fax: 914-876-2561; e-mail: HPHudson@aol.com.

Success in Newsletter Publishing; A Practical Guide, $39.50. Frederick D. Gross. Newsletter Association, 1401 Wilson Blvd., #403, Arlington, VA 22209; 800-356-9302.

Glossary

abstract   A brief description of chapters in a nonfiction book proposal (also called a **synopsis**); a point-by-point summary of an article or essay. In academic and technical journals, abstracts often appear with (and may serve to preface) the articles themselves.

acquisitions editor   An editor responsible for bringing in new books to publish.

advance   Money paid (usually in installments) to an author by a publisher prior to publication. The advance is paid against royalties: If an author is given a $5,000 advance, for instance, the author will collect royalties only after the monies due exceed $5,000. A good contract protects the advance if it exceeds the royalties that are ultimately due from sales.

advance orders   Orders received before a book's official publication date and sometimes before actual completion of the manufacture of the book.

agent   The person who acts on behalf of the author to handle the sale of literary properties. Good literary agents are as valuable to publishers as they are to writers; they select and present manuscripts appropriate for particular houses or of interest to particular acquisitions editors. Agents are paid on a percentage basis from the monies due their author clients.

American Society of Journalists and Authors   A membership organization for professional writers, ASJA provides a forum for information exchange among writers and others in the publishing community as well as for networking opportunities.

assignment editor   Staff member of a television or radio news team responsible for judging appropriateness of story ideas assigned to reporters for coverage.

assistants   The young, unsung folks who answer the phones, sort the mail, and otherwise keep publishing offices going.

auction   A sale usually conducted by an agent that gives several publishers the opportunity to bid on the rights to publish a book, with the book going to the highest bidder.

audience   That part of the population that will be interested in buying a specific book.

author   The writer of a book or books; the term usually implies a published writer.

author queries   A part of the editing process in which the editor and/or copy editor ask the author to further explain meaning, answer questions about accuracy or intent, or rewrite small sections.

author tour   Travel and promotional appearances by an author on behalf of the author's book.

authorized biography   A history of a person's life written with the authorization, cooperation, and, at times, participation of the subject or the subject's heirs.

author's copies/author's discount   Author's copies are the free copies of his or her book the author receives from the publisher; the exact number is stipulated in the contract, but it is usually at least ten hardcovers. The author will be able to purchase additional copies of the book (usually at a 40 percent discount from the retail price) and resell them at readings, lectures, and so on. If large quantities are bought, author's discounts can go as high as 70 percent.

autobiography   A history of a person's life written by that person or, as is typical, composed jointly with a collaborative writer ("as told to" or "with") or with a ghostwriter. Autobiographies by definition entail the full authorization, cooperation, participation, and ultimate approval of the subject.

backlist   Any book that has been in a bookstore for 90 days or more.

best-seller   Based on sales or orders by bookstores, wholesalers, and distributors, titles that move in the largest quantities. Lists of best-selling books can be local (newspapers), regional, national (*Publishers Weekly* or the *New York Times*), and international. Fiction and nonfiction are usually listed separately, as are hardcover and paperback volumes and sometimes additional classifications (such as how-to/self-improvement) are used; in addition, best-seller lists can be keyed to particular genres or specialty fields (such as best-seller lists for mysteries, science fiction, or romance novels, and for historical works, business books, or religious titles).

bibliography   A list of books, articles, and other sources that have been used in the writing of the text in which the bibliography appears. Complex works may break the bibliography down into discrete subject areas, such as general history, the twentieth century, or trade unions.

binding   The materials that hold a book together (including the cover). Bindings are generally denoted as hardcover (featuring heavy cardboard covered with durable cloth and/or paper) or paperback (using a pliable, resilient grade of paper). In the days when cloth was used more lavishly, hardcover volumes were conventionally known as clothbound; and in the very old days, hardcover bindings sometimes featured tooled leather and real gold- and silver-leaf ornamentation.

blues (or bluelines)   Photographic proofs of the printing plates for a book, used to inspect the set type, layout, and design before it goes to press.

blurb   A piece of written copy or extracted quotation used for publicity and promotional purposes, as on a flier, in a catalog, or in an advertisement.

boilerplate   A brief paragraph about the author, usually used as the first paragraph in a biography or last paragraph in a news release.

boilerplate contract   A publisher's standard contract before the author or agent requests modifications.

book club   A book-marketing organization that ships selected titles to subscribing members on a regular basis, sometimes at greatly reduced prices. Sales to book clubs are negotiated through the publisher's subsidiary rights department (in the case of a best-seller, the rights can be auctioned off). Terms vary, but the split of royalties between author and publisher is often 50/50. Book club sales are seen as blessed events by author, agent, and publisher alike.

book contract   A legally binding document that sets the terms for the advance, royalties, subsidiary rights, advertising, promotion, publicity, and a host of other contingencies and responsibilities. Writers should be thoroughly familiar with the concepts and terminology of the standard book-publishing contract.

book distribution   The method of getting books from the publisher's warehouse into the reader's hands—traditionally via bookstores but including such means as telemarketing and mail-order sales. Publishers use their own salesforce as well as independent salespeople, wholesalers, and distributors. Many large and some small publishers distribute for other publishers, which can be a good source of income. A publisher's distribution network is extremely important because it not only makes possible the vast sales of a best-seller but also affects the visibility of the publisher's entire list of books.

book expo   The annual publishing industry's trade show. It used to be called the ABA but now is the BEA, short for Book Expo America.

book producer or **book packager**   An individual or company that can assume many roles in the publishing process. A book packager or producer may conceive the idea for a book (most often nonfiction) or series, bring together the professionals (including the writer) needed to produce the book(s), sell the individual manuscript or series project to a publisher, take the project through to manufactured product—or perform any selection of those functions as commissioned by the publisher or other client (such as a corporation producing a corporate history as a premium or giveaway for employees and customers). The book producer may negotiate separate contracts with the publisher and with the writers, editors, and illustrators who contribute to the book.

book proposal   A packet of information about the writer's book idea. A proposal typically contains a solid description of the book's content, the potential market for the book, competition, and the author's credentials. It also contains a table of contents, an extensive book outline, and at least one sample chapter.

book review   A critical appraisal of a book (often reflecting a reviewer's personal opinion or recommendation) that evaluates such aspects as organization and writing style, possible market appeal, and cultural, political, or literary significance. Before the public reads book reviews in the local and national print media, important reviews have been published in such respected trade journals as *Publishers Weekly, Kirkus Reviews, Library Journal,* and *Booklist.* A rave review from one of these journals will encourage booksellers to order the book; copies of these raves will be used for promotion and publicity purposes by the publisher and will encourage other book reviewers nationwide to review the book.

booker   The staff person at a TV, radio, or cable station who responds to pitch letters when an appearance needs to be arranged or "booked."

Books in Print Listings, published by R. R. Bowker, of books currently in print. These annual volumes (along with periodic supplements such as *Forthcoming Books in Print*) provide ordering information, including titles, authors, ISBN numbers, prices, whether a book is available in hardcover or paperback, and publisher names. Intended for use by the book trade, *Books in Print* is also of great value to writers who are researching the markets for their projects. Listings are provided alphabetically by author, title, and subject area.

bound galleys Copies of uncorrected typesetter's page proofs or printouts of electronically produced mechanicals that are bound together as advance copies of the book. Bound galleys are sent to trade journals as well as to a limited number of major reviewers who work under long lead times.

broadcast Electronically transmit by radio or television.

bulk sales The discounted sale of many copies of a single title (the greater the number of books, the larger the discount).

buzz The word-of-mouth excitement created in the publishing community before a book is released.

byline The name of the author of a piece, indicating credit for having written a book or article. Ghostwriters, by definition, do not receive bylines.

camera-ready art The finished artwork that is ready to be photographed, without alteration, for reproduction.

chapter book A category of children's books that has longer stories and are written for the intermediate reader.

client pays wire service Client pays to have her own news or feature stories transmitted through print and broadcast media newsrooms at no cost to the media.

clip or **clippings** A story cut from a publication or a segment cut from a videotape or audiotape.

clip art Artwork specifically designed to be used by anyone without obtaining permission.

coauthor One who shares authorship of a work. Coauthors have bylines and share royalties based on their contribution to the work.

collaboration A writer's working jointly with professionals in any number of fields to produce books outside the writer's own areas of expertise (for example, a writer with an interest in exercise and nutrition may collaborate with a doctor on a health book). Though the writer may be billed as a coauthor, the writer does not necessarily receive a byline (in which case the writer is a ghostwriter), and royalties are shared based on respective contributions to the book (including expertise, promotional abilities, and the actual writing).

commission The percentage of the advance and subsequent royalties that an agent receives as his fee after selling a writer's work to a publisher. It can run anywhere from 10 to 25 percent (the larger percentages are for subrights).

community coordinator (See **events coordinator.**)

compositor   A person who designs and typesets manuscripts and then prepares formatted disks that are sent to the printer.

concept stories   Feature stories designed to pique the interest of a certain demographic audience.

contributing reporter or **writer**   Term often used to describe freelance writers.

copy editor   An editor responsible for the final polishing of a manuscript who reads primarily to ensure appropriate word usage and grammatical expression, clarity, and coherence of the material as presented in addition to correcting factual errors and inconsistencies, spelling, and punctuation.

copyright   The legal proprietary right to reproduce, have reproduced, publish, and sell copies of literary, musical, and other artistic works. The rights to literary properties belong to the authors from the time the work is produced regardless of whether a formal copyright registration is obtained. However, for legal recourse in the event of plagiarism, the work must be registered with the U.S. Copyright Office, and all copies of the work must bear the copyright notice.

corporate fact sheet   A one-page document that describes a company's principals, services, philosophy, and fees. Includes address, telephone, fax and e-mail address, and map to allow prospective clients or reporters to easily find a business.

counter display   Several copies of a book in a cardboard holder for display in a bookstore; also called a "counter pack."

cover blurbs   Favorable quotes from other writers, celebrities, or experts in a book's subject area that appear on a book jacket and are used to enhance the book's point-of-purchase appeal to potential book buyers.

deadline   Not-so-subtle synonym for an author's due date for submission of a completed manuscript to the publisher, which can be as much as a full year before the official publication date unless the book is being produced quickly to coincide with, or follow up, a particular event.

delivery   Submission of a completed manuscript to the editor or publisher.

demographics   Population statistics, age groups, buying habits, personal income levels, and other categories that can be used to estimate a book's potential success.

display titles   Books produced to be eye-catching to the casual browser in a bookstore. Often rich with splashy cover art, these publications are intended to pique the bookbuyer's senses. Many display titles are stacked on their own freestanding racks; a book shelved with its front cover showing is technically a display title. Promotional or premium titles are likely to be display items, as are mass-market paperbacks and hardbacks with enormous best-seller potential.

distributor   An agent or business that buys books from a publisher to resell, at a higher cost, to wholesalers, retailers, or individuals. Skillful use of distribution networks can give a small publisher greater national visibility.

dubs   Copies of TV or radio appearances on videotape or audiotape.

dump   Publishing industry slang for a counter display (see above). Dumps are usually the larger cardboard displays that stand on the floor.

dust jacket   (also dustcover or book jacket) The paper wrapper that covers the binding of hardcover books designed especially for the book by either the publisher's art department or a freelance artist. Dust jackets were originally conceived to protect books during shipping, but now their function is primarily promotional—to entice browsers to reach out and pick up the volume—by means of attractive graphics and sizzling promotional copy.

easy readers   A category of children's books that refers to storybooks with short, simple sentences designed for beginning readers.

editor   Editorial responsibilities and titles vary from house to house (usually being less strictly defined in smaller houses). In general, the duties of the editor in chief or executive editor are primarily administrative: managing personnel, scheduling, budgeting, and defining the editorial personality of the firm or imprint. Senior editors and acquisitions editors acquire manuscripts (and authors), conceive project ideas and find writers to carry them out, and may oversee the writing and rewriting of manuscripts. Managing editors have editorial and production responsibilities, coordinating and scheduling the book through the various phases of production. Associate and assistant editors edit; they are involved in most of the rewriting and reshaping of a manuscript. Copy editors read the manuscript and style its punctuation, grammar, spelling, headings and subheadings, and the like. Editorial assistants, laden with extensive clerical duties, perform some editorial duties as well—often as springboards to senior editorial positions.

editorial   A statement of opinion from an editor or publisher about you and your business. Media coverage generated by news staff.

editorial board   The group of people who collectively make the decision to publish. Acquisitions editors present book proposals to the editorial board for its approval; sometimes called a "pub board."

editorial calendar   The listing of specific times a publication will focus on special sections or special news reporting.

endcap   The shelf at the end of an aisle in a bookstore. Publishers can sometimes pay booksellers for the chance to display their books on the endcap.

endnotes   Explanatory notes and/or source citations that appear either at the end of individual chapters or at the end of a book's text; used primarily in scholarly or academically oriented works.

English cozy   A type of mystery book set in England that often features a quaint English atmosphere.

epilogue   The final segment of a book, which comes "after the end." In both fiction and nonfiction, an epilogue offers commentary or further information but does not bear directly on the book's central design.

events coordinator A bookstore employee, called a community coordinator, sometimes responsible for arranging author signings, author appearances, and in-store events.

exclusive A news item or feature article that only one newspaper, magazine, or television station may carry.

exclusive submission A proposal that only one agent or editor is considering.

F&Gs Sheets of paper "folded and gathered" in preparation for printing. This is another test step that publishers can review and approve before seeing finished, bound books.

face out Books placed on a store's shelf with the cover facing out toward the customer.

feature A special story or article in a print publication or broadcast program that goes into detail about concepts and ideas of specific market interest.

featured guest A guest that is central to a television show's segment. If a number of experts are used on the same show, the guest is a panel member rather than the focus of the show.

fiction Literary works of the imagination.

first printing The number of books printed in the initial print run.

first serial An excerpt that appears in a newspaper or magazine prior to a book's publication and actual release.

floor The minimum bid in an auction.

footnotes Explanatory notes and/or source citations that appear at the bottom of a page. Footnotes are rare in general-interest books, the preferred style being either to work such information into the text or to list informational sources in the bibliography.

foreword An introductory piece written by an author or an expert in the given field. A foreword by a celebrity or well-respected authority is a strong selling point for a prospective project or, after publication, for the book itself.

formatting The set of instructions that determines the way that the printed words appear on the page, including such things as margins, indentations, type size, and type font.

freelance A writer who sells writing services and is not under regular contract to any one publication.

frequency The number of times any publication comes out in a given period of time (i.e., daily, weekly, quarterly, etc.).

front matter The first several pages of a book that typically contain the half-title page, the title page, copyright information, the dedication, acknowledgments, and the table of contents. Front matter pages are numbered *i, ii, iii, iv,* and so forth, using roman numerals.

frontlist Books that have just been published.

fulfillment house   A firm commissioned to fill orders for a publisher; services may include warehousing, shipping, receiving returns, and mail-order and direct marketing response. Although more common for magazine publishers, fulfillment houses also serve book publishers.

galleys   Printer's proofs (or copies of proofs) on sheets of paper, or printouts of the electronically produced setup of a book's interior. These represent the author's last chance to check for typos and make any (usually minimal) revisions or additions to the copy. (See **bound galleys.**)

genre fiction   A term applied to romance, sci-fi, and horror novels, Westerns, thrillers, and fantasy novels.

ghostwriter   A writer without a byline and often without the remuneration and recognition that credited authors receive. Ghostwriters typically get flat fees for their work, but even without royalties, experienced ghosts can receive respectable sums.

glossary   An alphabetical listing of special terms as they are used in a particular subject area, often with more in-depth explanations than would be provided by general dictionary definitions.

hardcover   Books bound in a format that uses thick, sturdy, relatively stiff binding boards and a cover composed (usually) of a cloth spine and finished binding paper. Hardcover books are conventionally wrapped in a dust jacket. (See **binding, dust jacket.**)

head   The title introducing a chapter or subdivision of text.

hook   The distinctive concept or theme of a work that sets it apart as being fresh, new, or different from others in its field. A hook can be an author's special point of view, often encapsulated in a catchy or provocative phrase intended to attract or pique the interest of a reader, editor, or agent. One important function of a hook is to present what might otherwise be seen as dry, though significant, subject matter as an exciting, commercially attractive package (academic or scientific topics; number-crunching drudgery, such as home bookkeeping).

how-to books   An immensely popular category of books ranging from the purely instructional (arts and crafts, for example) to the motivational (popular psychology, self-improvement, inspirational) to get-rich-quick advice (real estate and investment).

illustrated books   A category of children's books that have lots of pictures and few words.

imprint   A separate product line within a publishing house. Imprints may be composed of just one or two series or may offer large, diversified lists. Imprints enjoy varying degrees of autonomy from the parent company. An imprint may have its own editorial department (possibly consisting of only one editor), or house acquisitions editors may assign particular titles for release on appropriate specialized imprints. An imprint may publish a certain kind of book (juvenile or paperback or travel) or have its own personality (such as a literary tone).

in print   Books that are currently available from the publisher. Should a publisher decide to discontinue publishing a title, it goes out of print and is no longer available.

independent booksellers   Locally owned and operated bookstores not affiliated with a large chain such as Borders or Barnes and Noble.

index   An alphabetical directory at the end of a book that references names and subjects discussed in the book and the pages where such mentions can be found.

instant book   A book that appears on bookstore shelves just weeks after the event that is the focus of the book.

intellectual property   According to *Random House Legal Dictionary*, "copyrights, patents, and other rights in creations of the mind; also, the creations themselves, such as a literary work, painting, or computer program."

introduction   Preliminary remarks pertaining to a work. Like a foreword, an introduction can be written by the author or an appropriate authority on the subject. If a book has both a foreword and an introduction, the foreword will be written by someone other than the author; the introduction will be more closely tied to the text and will be written by the book's author. (See **foreword.**)

ISBN (International Standard Book Number)   A ten-digit number that identifies the title and publisher of a book. It is used for ordering and cataloging books and appears on all dustcovers, on the back cover of books, and on the copyright page.

lead   The crucial first few sentences of a query letter, book proposal, novel, news release, article, advertisement, or sales-tip sheet in which the writer must hook the reader, consumer, editor, or agent.

lead time   The period of time reporters and producers need to prepare stories and information for publication or broadcast.

lead title   A frontlist book featured by a publisher during a given season—one the publisher believes should do extremely well commercially. Lead titles are usually those given the publisher's maximum promotional push.

letterpress   A form of printing in which set type is inked, then impressed directly onto the printing surface. Now used primarily for limited-run books-as-fine-art projects. (Compare **offset.**)

letters to the editor   Your opportunity to congratulate, discuss, or criticize an article you have read.

Library of Congress   The largest library in the world, in Washington, D.C. As part of its many services, the Library of Congress will supply a writer with up-to-date sources and bibliographies in all fields, from arts and humanities to science and technology. For details, write to the Library of Congress, Central Services Division, Washington, DC 20540.

Library of Congress catalog card number   An identifying number issued by the Library of Congress to books it has accepted for its collection. The publication of those books, which are submitted by the publishers, are announced by the Library of Congress to libraries, which use Library of Congress numbers for their own ordering and cataloging purposes.

list   A publisher's list of forthcoming titles; that is, the books it plans to publish in the coming season or year.

live show   A television or radio show that is broadcast at the same moment it is happening.

manuscript guidelines   A publisher's rules regarding the proper way to prepare manuscripts for submission.

mass-market paperback   Less expensive, smaller-format paperbacks that are sold from racks (in such venues as supermarkets, variety stores, drugstores, and specialty shops) as well as in bookstores. Also referred to as rack editions.

masthead   A list of editors, publishers, and senior reporters in each publication's issue; includes an address and telephone number.

mechanicals   Finished pages ready to be sent to the printer.

media   Reporters, editors, and producers of print publications, broadcast programs, and online magazines.

media market   A geographic area covered by a particular radio station, TV channel, or newspaper. Some markets, such as New York, are large media markets; others are small.

media outlet   Any publication or broadcast program that transmits news and feature stories to the public through any distribution channel.

memoir   An account of the events in the author's own life.

midlist   Books that are acquired for modest advances, given modest print runs, and have a relatively short shelf life.

morning drive time   A radio term referring to broadcasts between the hours of 6:00 AM and 9:00 AM, while commuters are headed to work.

multiple queries   When more than one agent or editor is approached at the same time about a book idea.

network   A chain of broadcast or radio stations controlled and operated as a unit, often using the same editorial material.

nonfiction   Works that contain true information or observation.

op-ed   An article written by an expert that is positioned on the page opposite the editorial page of a newspaper. Not to be confused with Letters to the Editor.

option clause/right of first refusal   In a book contract, a clause that stipulates that the publisher will have the right to publish the author's next book. However, the publisher is under no obligation to do so.

out of print   (See **in print.**)

outline   A hierarchical listing of topics that provides the writer (and the proposal reader) with an overview of a book's ideas in the order in which they will be presented; used for both a book proposal and the actual writing and structuring of a book.

overview A one-sentence description of a book and its audience; a Hollywood term now leaking into the book world.

P & L A profit and loss statement prepared by an editor in advance of acquiring a book.

page count The number of book pages. Sometimes, the minimum (or maximum) number of pages in a completed manuscript is stipulated in the book contract.

panel member (See **featured guest.**)

parody A comic imitation of a well-known literary work.

payment on publication A term meaning that the writer is not paid until the work actually appears in print. This is the policy of many magazine publishers and some book publishers.

periodicals Publications circulated at such regular intervals as weekly or monthly.

permission The right to quote or reprint published material obtained by the author from the copyright holder.

pitch letter A letter written to introduce a source and story idea to a member of the media.

placements Stories or mentions of an author or book in the media resulting from publicity efforts.

platform An author's proven ability to promote and sell his or her book through public speaking, a television or radio show, or a newspaper column.

preface An element of a book's front matter. In the preface, the author may discuss the purpose of the book, the type of research on which it is based, its genesis, or its underlying philosophy.

prepack Several copies of a book offered at a special discount and placed together in a cardboard display.

press conference A meeting to which members of the press are invited to hear something newsworthy.

press kit A promotional package that includes a press release, tip sheet, author biography and photograph, reviews, and other pertinent information. The press kit can be put together by the publisher's publicity department or an independent publicist and sent with a review copy of the book to potential reviewers and to media professionals responsible for booking author appearances.

price Several prices pertain to a single book—the invoice price is the amount the publisher charges the bookseller; the retail, cover, or list price is what the consumer pays.

print run The number of books printed each time a book goes to press.

producer The person in charge of the coordination of all details inherent in a television or radio program.

promotion   Free publicity methods and/or paid advertising for a book or its author to create public awareness and stimulate sales.

proposal   A detailed presentation of a book's concept used to gain the interest and services of an agent and to sell the project to a publisher.

public domain   Material that is uncopyrighted, whose copyright has expired, or is uncopyrightable. The last category includes government publications, jokes, titles, and, it should be remembered, ideas.

publication date (or **pub date**)   A book's official date of publication, customarily set by the publisher to fall six weeks after completed bound books are delivered to the warehouse. The publication date is used to schedule the promotional activities on behalf of the title so that books will have had time to be ordered, shipped, and received in stores to coincide with the appearance of advertising and publicity.

publications   Newspapers, magazines, and newsletters with information, news, and feature stories, usually produced to be sold or as a service to members of associations or organizations.

publicist (press agent)   The professional who handles press releases for new books and arranges the author's publicity tour.

publicity   Attention directed to a book or its author. Publicity is usually free and includes book reviews, feature articles, television and radio appearances or interviews, and online mentions.

publisher's catalog   A seasonal sales catalog that lists and describes a publisher's new books; it is sent to all potential buyers, including individuals who request one. Catalogs range from the basic to the glitzy and often include information about authors, print quantity, and the amount of money slated to be spent on publicity and promotion.

publisher's discount   The percentage by which a publisher discounts the retail price of a book to a bookseller, often based in part on the number of copies purchased.

Publisher's Weekly (PW)   The publishing industry's chief trade journal. *PW* carries announcements of upcoming books, respected book reviews, interviews with authors, and news (such as mergers and personnel changes).

query letter   A brief written presentation to an agent or editor designed to pitch both the writer and the book idea.

reach   The geographic area of the audience and the numbers of readers, listeners, or viewers who can access the media in any region.

readers   The method by which university presses evaluate projects. Readers, or "referees," who are experts in a specific field are paid to read and pass judgment on the scholarship of a proposed work.

reading fees   A fee requested by an agent to pay for the time he spends reading a writer's project to decide if it is worth representing.

rejection letter   A formal "no thanks" letter from an agent or an editor in passing on a project.

remainders   Unsold book stock. Remainders may include titles that have not sold as well as anticipated in addition to unsold copies of later printings of best-sellers. These volumes are often remaindered—that is, remaining stock is purchased from the publisher at a huge discount and resold to the public.

reprint   A subsequent edition of material that is already in print, especially publication in a different format—the paperback reprint of a hardcover, for example.

résumé   A summary of an individual's employment experience and education. When a résumé is sent to prospective agents or publishers, it should contain the author's publishing credits, specialty credentials, and pertinent personal experiences. Also referred to as a curriculum vitae or, more simply, vita.

returns   Unsold books returned to a publisher by a bookstore, for which the store may receive full or partial credit (depending on the publisher's policy, the age of the book, and so on).

reversion-of-rights clause   In a book contract, a clause stating that if the book goes out of print or the publisher fails to reprint the book within a stipulated length of time, all rights revert to the author.

review copy   A free copy of a (usually) new book sent to print and electronic media that review books for their audiences.

round-up story   A story geared to look back at what has happened over a specific period, such as the previous year or quarter. A story for which a reporter wants five or ten opinions on a subject.

royalty   The percentage of a book's retail cost that is paid to the author for each copy sold after the author's advance has been recouped by the publisher. Some publishers structure royalties as a percentage payment against net receipts.

sales conference   A publisher's semiannual meeting of its editorial and sales departments and senior promotion and publicity staff members, during which the upcoming season's new books are introduced and marketing strategies are discussed.

sales representative (sales rep)   A member of a publisher's salesforce or an independent contractor who, armed with a book catalog and order forms, visits bookstores in a certain territory to sell books to retailers.

SASE (self-addressed stamped envelope)   It is customary for an author to enclose SASEs with query letters, proposals, and manuscript submissions. Many editors and agents don't reply if a writer has neglected to enclose an SASE.

seasons   Publishers put together their lists of books and their catalogs according to two or three seasons: fall, winter, and spring.

second serial   Excerpts from a book that are published after the book is published and available.

self-publishing   A publishing project wherein an author pays the costs of manufacturing and selling his or her own book and retains all profits from the book's sales. This is a risky venture but can be profitable (especially when combined with an author's speaking engagements or imaginative marketing techniques); in addition, self-publication, if successful, can lead to distribution or publication by a commercial publisher. (Compare with **subsidy publishing**.)

sell-through   Books that have actually been purchased at the bookstore level and are not going to be returned unsold to the publisher.

sequel   A second book that features many of the same characters as the first book.

serial rights   Reprint rights sold to periodicals. First serial rights include the right to publish the material before anyone else (generally before the book is released or coinciding with the book's official publication) within either the United States or a wider territory. Second serial rights cover material already published either in a book or in another periodical.

series   Books linked by a brand-name identity or linked in theme, purpose, or content.

shelf life   The amount of time an unsold book remains on a bookstore shelf before the store manager pulls it to make room for newer incoming stock with greater (or at least untested) sales potential.

sidebar   A legal term that the media adopted to describe a portion of a story that is relevant, but not necessary, to the body of the story, such as data, a glossary, or a deeper explanation of a concept mentioned in the story. Usually, it is set apart in a box, margin, or shaded area, or set in smaller type to distinguish it from the rest of the text on the page.

signature   A group of book pages that have been printed together on one large sheet of paper that is then folded and cut in preparation for being bound, along with the book's other signatures, into the final volume.

simultaneous publication   The issuing at the same time of more than one edition of a work, such as in hardcover and trade paperback. Simultaneous releases may be expanded to include mass-market paper versions and, rarely, deluxe gift editions.

simultaneous (or multiple) submissions   The submission of the same material to more than one publisher at the same time. Although simultaneous submission is a common practice, publishers should always be told when it is being done. Multiple submissions by an author to several agents is, on the other hand, a practice that is often frowned on by agents.

slush pile   The morass of unsolicited manuscripts at a publishing house or literary agency, which may fester indefinitely awaiting (perhaps perfunctory) review. Some publishers or agencies do not maintain slush piles. Unsolicited manuscripts are slated for instant return without review (if an SASE is included) or may otherwise be literally or figuratively pitched to the wind. Querying a targeted publisher or agent before submitting a manuscript is an excellent way of avoiding, or at least minimizing, the possibility of such an ignoble fate.

small publisher   A general term that is applied to publishing houses with revenues of less than $10 million a year. It is also sometimes called a small press.

specialized publications   Industry-specific trade or professional publications (manufacturing, insurance, telecommunications, etc.).

spin   Jargon for the point of view or bias you create in a story.

spine The portion of a book's casing (or binding) that backs the bound signatures and is visible when the volume is aligned on a bookshelf.

spine out A book that is placed on a bookstore shelf with only the spine showing.

stamping In book publishing, the impression of ornamental type and images (such as logo) on the book's binding by using a die with raised or intaglio surface to apply ink or metallic-leaf stamping.

stand-up shot A news source filmed standing in front of a wall while a TV reporter asks questions. This kind of shot adds an authoritative slant to a television story.

submission The process by which a writer or agent submits a book proposal or manuscript to a publisher. If the author is not using an agent, it is called an "un-agented submission."

subsidiary rights The reprint, serial, movie, television, audiotape, and videotape rights deriving from a book. The division of profits between publisher and author from the sales of these rights is determined through negotiation. In more elaborately commercial projects, such details as syndication of related articles and licensing of characters may ultimately be involved.

subsidy publishing A mode of publication wherein the author pays a publishing company to produce his or her work, which may thus appear superficially to have been conventionally published. Subsidy publishing (also known as vanity publishing) is generally more expensive than self-publishing because the subsidy house makes a profit on all its contracted functions, charging fees well beyond basic costs for production and services.

syndicated Reports that appear in more than one media outlet simultaneously.

syndicated column Material published simultaneously in a number of newspapers or magazines. The author shares the income from syndication with the syndicate that negotiates the sale.

syndicated columnist A person hired by publications or broadcast organizations to produce written or spoken commentary about specific feature subjects.

synopsis A summary in paragraph form rather than in outline format. The synopsis is an important part of a book proposal. For fiction, the synopsis hits the key points of the plot. In a nonfiction book proposal, the synopsis describes the thrust and content of the successive chapters (and/or parts) of the manuscript.

talking head The television shot that shows only the upper shoulders, neck, and face of the person being interviewed. Usually accompanied by a computer-generated sign that appears midchest identifying the person and his or her company.

taped show A television or radio show that is not broadcast immediately but at a later date.

text Words on a page are called text. This distinguishes them from artwork.

trade books Books distributed through the book trade—meaning bookstores and major book clubs—as opposed to, for example, mass-market paperbacks, which are also sold at magazine racks, newsstands, and supermarkets.

trade discount   The discount from the cover or list price that a publisher gives the bookseller. It is usually proportional to the number of books ordered (the larger the order, the greater the discount) and is typically between 40 and 50 percent.

trade list   A catalog of all of a publisher's books in print, with ISBNs and order information. The trade list sometimes includes descriptions of the current season's new books.

trade paperback   Any paperback book of any size other than the 4½-by-7-inch "mass market"–size books.

trade publishers   Publishers of books for general readership—that is, nonprofessional, nonacademic books that are distributed primarily through bookstores.

university press   A publishing house affiliated with a sponsoring university. The press is generally nonprofit and subsidized by the university. Generally, university presses publish noncommercial scholarly nonfiction books written by academics, though their lists may include literary fiction, criticism, and poetry. Some university presses also specialize in titles of regional interest, and many acquire limited numbers of projects intended for broader commercial appeal.

unsolicited manuscript   A manuscript sent to an editor or agent that has not been requested by the editor/agent.

vanity press   A publisher that publishes books only at an author's expense—and will generally agree to publish virtually anything that is submitted and paid for. (See **subsidy publishing.**)

video clip   A tape of an author's television appearance.

wire service   News stories, features, and the like sent by direct line to subscribing or member newspapers and radio and television stations.

writing coach   A professional writer who coaches inexperienced writers through the writing process to make their material commercial.

word count   The number of words in a document. When noted on a manuscript, the word count is usually rounded off to the nearest 100 words.

work-for-hire agreement   An arrangement in which a writer is paid one time for his or her work. Under a work-for-hire agreement, the writer does not own the copyright and receives no royalties.

Index

Credibility Marketing

For special discounts on 20 or more copies of *Credibility Marketing: Build Your Business by Becoming a Recognized Expert (Without Investing a Lot of Time or Money)*, please call Dearborn Trade Special Sales at 800-621-9621, extension 4307.

Dearborn™
Trade Publishing
A **Kaplan Professional** Company